NAVMC 2750

MARINES

WAR ON DRUGS

PCN 100 013439 00

DEPARTMENT OF THE NAVY
HEADQUARTERS UNITED STATES MARINE CORPS
WASHINGTON, D.C. 20380

IN REPLY REFER TO

NAVMC 2750
MPH-40B-eb-B
21 May 1982

FOREWORD

1. PURPOSE

This publication, NAVMC 2750, Marines War on Drugs, is designed as a basic reference for use by commanders in developing local illegal drug use prevention and instructional programs.

2. SCOPE

NAVMC 2750 does not amend nor change existing directives, orders or policy of this or higher authority; if conflicts arise, published directives and/or orders take precedence.

3. SUPERSESSION

None

4. ADDITIONAL COPIES

Additional copies may be obtained from the Marine Corps publication stock point at Marine Corps Logistics Base, Albany, Georgia, in accordance with the provisions of MCO P5600.31.

5. CERTIFICATION

Reviewed and approved this date.

A. LUKEMAN
Brigadier General, U.S. Marine Corps
Director, Manpower Plans and Policy Division

DISTRIBUTION: A (5 COPIES EACH ADEE)

Copy to: 8145001

PREFACE

"First to fight for right and freedom,
And to keep our honor clean."
---- THE MARINES' HYMN

Since 1775 the United States Marine Corps has enjoyed the reputation of an elite, disciplined, well-trained fighting force. This kind of reputation must be earned every day. It is founded upon the unfailing trust of one Marine in another, unwavering confidence in teamwork, and the dogged determination of unit leaders to meet the challenges at hand.

We are at war. The enemy is illegal drug use. It threatens both our Corps and our society and is more devastating than a holocaust, more debilitating than disease.

Marines must again rise to the challenge. They must be the driving force in the war to eliminate illegal drug use in our Corps. Marine leaders must "take the point" in this campaign.

CONTENTS

Users of this NAVMC are encouraged to submit recommended changes or comments to improve it to Commandant of the Marine Corps (Code MPH-40), Headquarters, U.S. Marine Corps, Washington, D.C. 20380.

Comments should be keyed to specific page, paragraph and line of text in which the change is recommended.

INTRODUCTION

"The distribution, possession or use of illegal drugs
is not tolerated in the United States Marine Corps."
        General Robert H. BARROW
        Commandant, U. S. Marine Corps

We as leaders of Marines have been concerned with
illegal drug use related problems for more than a decade.
Unfortunately, our previous efforts to stem illegal drug
use have been generally unsuccessful, and it is naive for
any Marine leader to think otherwise. In short, we are at
war with illegal drugs and we have not been winning. With
this in mind, the Commandant has directed a campaign
against illegal drug use. The objective is eliminating
illegal drug use in our Corps.

Unlike previous efforts and programs, characterized
mostly by education and rehabilitation, our new plan of
attack emphasizes leadership, enforcement of standards,
identification and education. Paramount to the success of
this war on drugs is a total leadership effort involving
the full participation of all officers, staff noncommissioned officers and noncommissioned officers.

Marine Corps leadership at all levels must be thoroughly
knowledgeable about the drug problem, the detrimental
impact that drug use has on unit readiness, individual
performance and mission accomplishment, and measures to
combat use of illegal drugs. Most importantly, Marine
Corps leaders must be capable of convincing Marines in
their charge that the use of illegal drugs is
fundamentally wrong and destructive to organizational
effectiveness.

This publication is designed as a basic reference for Marine
Corps programs to eliminate illegal drug use within the Marine
Corps. Chapter I defines the extent of the problem, focusing on
the most significant considerations: why Marines illegally use
drugs; the adverse impact of such use on readiness; and the leader's
responsibility in eliminating illegal drug use in the Corps.
Chapter II presents factual information concerning drugs and their
illegal use, enabling leaders to separate "fact" from "fiction".
and to become more knowledgeable in such matters as terminology,

paraphernalia, and illegal drug use methods. Chapter III
provides the key considerations for developing an effective
illegal drug use program with the objective being the
elimination of illegal drug use. Chapter IV outlines the
full spectrum of actions, both administrative and legal,
available to the leader in combating illegal drug use.
In addition, a selective listing of currently available
films and publications is provided. Finally, the outlines
of each of the first four chapters facilitate instructor
presentation of the information. In essence, this NAVMC
is one of your weapons in the war against illegal drug use.

WAR ON DRUGS CHAPTER I

THE PROBLEM

"I have treated the subject with too much naivete...."
General Robert H. Barrow
Commandant, U. S. Marine Corps

This chapter presents facts concerning illegal drug use in American society and in the United States Marine Corps. It also addresses why Marines abuse drugs and how that abuse impacts on unit readiness. In short, it focuses on "The Problem", which active and enlightened leadership can help solve.

DRUGS IN SOCIETY

Historically, mankind has always used drugs; the reasons are basically unchanging: to alleviate pain and discomfort; to relieve boredom; to escape stress and pressures; to create a sense of euphoria; and to enhance social interactions.

Hashish, opium, cocaine, and other drugs that affect behavior have been used since antiquity to induce intoxication during religious rites, to prepare warriors for battle or to use medicinally as pain relievers. They were known to the ancient Chinese, the Egyptians and the Greeks mainly for their therapeutic value, but even then they were used by some as agents of indulgence.

Opium and its derivatives have the power to allay anxiety, gloom, and despair, as well as to provide escape from boredom and loneliness—even from reality itself. Despite its wide medicinal use, the medical profession did not understand opium's addictive liability until the late 1800's. Its legality and inexpensive availability during the post-Civil War era led to an extensive addiction problem in American society.

The final link in the opiate chain was forged in 1898 when heroin, a morphine derivative, was synthesized. It too was eventually considered nonaddictive and was easily obtained in any pharmacy. By 1900 opiate indulgence in America cut across economic and social lines. Whatever the initiating cause, it seems probable that most users turned to narcotics to escape physical or emotional pain, then gradually became addicted.

In recent years, public attention has been increasingly focused on the abuse of non-narcotic drugs such as amphetamines (stimulants), barbiturates (sedatives), hallucinogens, tranquilizers and marijuana. From 1968 to the present, this type of illegal drug use has grown at an alarming rate throughout the world, but especially in the United States. In part, this may reflect the public's association of non-narcotic drugs with occasional or recreational use, the social acceptance and widespread use of amphetamines and barbiturates in legitimate medical therapy, and the availability of such drugs from other than underworld contacts. Also, while the dangers of narcotic addiction are acknowledged, the inherent dangers in many non-narcotics have not been generally recognized. The result is that during the last two decades illegal drug use has spread to the extent that it is not an unusual occurrence in any social or economic strata in the United States. Exposure to illegal drugs is so commonplace in the American lifestyle, particularly among young persons, that the decision to try them is viewed the same as older generations' experimentation with tobacco and alcohol.

Contact with illegal drugs is routinely made by young people before the tenth grade. Surveys of high school students indicate nearly forty percent regularly use drugs, and almost ten percent use them on a daily basis. Studies also indicate illegal drug use is prevalent in American society in persons ages eighteen to twenty-five.... NOTE: Over eighty percent of Marine active duty enlisted personnel are twenty-five or younger.

DRUGS IN THE MARINE CORPS

A DoD worldwide drug and alcohol survey, published in November, 1980, compared the amount of illegal drug use in the military: the Air Force was lowest, while the Marine Corps was the highest. In fact, one test indicated more Marines between the ages of eighteen and twenty-five were using marijuana and other drugs than any of the other services, and even more than civilians of equal ages! Forty-seven percent of Marine enlisted men and women, privates through sergeant, claimed they had used marijuana or hash within thirty days prior to the survey. Even more alarming was the five percent of staff NCOs, the five percent of company grade officers, and the two percent of the field grade officers admitting to marijuana use within thirty days of the survey.

IMPACT OF ILLEGAL DRUG USE

Substance abuse has a decided impact on individual performance. Marines who are psychologically and physiologically drug dependent or under the influence of drugs are not reliable. They have difficulty completing physical tasks requiring stamina and endurance, as well as those requiring precision and judgement. Social behavior also suffers from drug abuse. In the DoD survey on illegal drug use, fifteen percent of those surveyed admitted to having disciplinary problems, accidents, increased marital, and/or financial difficulties as a direct result of their drug use. Obviously, illegal drug use degrades the individual self-discipline, motivation and performance of too many of our Marines.

In the Marine Corps, mission accomplishment is based on teamwork. It is evident that the better the teamwork, the better the mission will be performed. Illegal drug users are poor team members; in fact, they are liabilities - they are accidents and mistakes waiting to happen! The possible consequences of Marines performing duty under the influence of drugs provide specters that no reasonable leader can deny: infantrymen who are too debilitated to reach the objective; artillery men who miscount powder increments; warehousemen who misplace inventory; mechanics who mis-torque settings; avionics technicians who do not worry about finite calibrations; and firewatches and security watches who "nod off" on duty. Such situations and incidents not only degrade mission readiness, THEY ADVERSELY AFFECT THE SAFETY AND WELL-BEING OF MARINES. We will not tolerate illegal drug users.

LEADERSHIP CHALLENGE

Young men and women from across America enter the Corps with certain values, attitudes and predispositions about drugs. During initial training, many of those are changed as the new Marines are indoctrinated with values consistent with the high standards of the Corps: individual and unit pride, desire for excellence, self-discipline, physical fitness, esprit, and un-swerving loyalty to Country and Corps. Recruits quickly learn that association with illegal drugs is contradictory to Marine values. Illegal drugs are strictly forbidden, and Marines using them will be disciplined and separated from the Corps.

Our challenge as leaders is to continue the education and the motivation Marines receive during initial training. Through intelligent leadership, education, early identification of the illegal drug user, and strict enforcement of standards, we are reinforcing an attitude of intolerance toward illegal drug use and nurturing the spirit of unit integrity based on a truly ready, drug free, band of brothers. Leaders at all levels are involved.

WAR ON DRUGS CHAPTER II

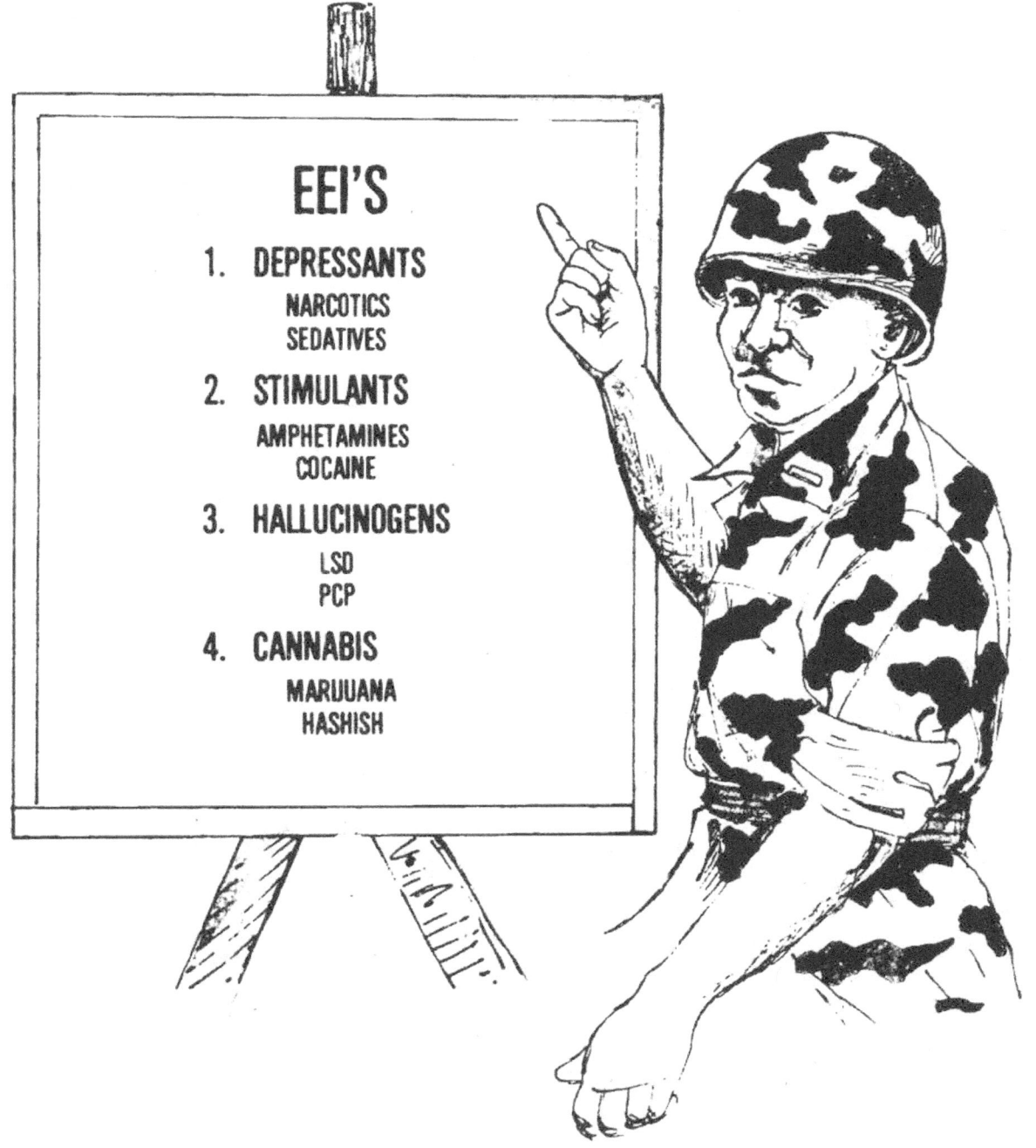

EEI'S

1. **DEPRESSANTS**
   NARCOTICS
   SEDATIVES

2. **STIMULANTS**
   AMPHETAMINES
   COCAINE

3. **HALLUCINOGENS**
   LSD
   PCP

4. **CANNABIS**
   MARIJUANA
   HASHISH

CLASSIFICATIONS

"...the grunts had stampeded past him, racing toward oblivion, the juicers popping open cans of Carling Black Label, the smokers ripping up the barracks floorboards to get at their stashes of el-primo no-seed, no-stem marijuana laid in at $50 the 6-pound sandbag full."

CHARLIE COMPANY, THE BIG RED ONE
NEWSWEEK/December 14, 1981

INTRODUCTION

Enlightened Marine leaders are essential to an effective drug prevention program. They must see to it that all Marines are thoroughly educated concerning the ill-effects of illegal drug use. This chapter covers the categories and effects of drugs, related terminology, and common paraphernalia associated with illegal drug use. It should help Marines recognize the facts about illegal drug use, and discard ill-perceived popular myths.

GENERAL CLASSIFICATIONS OF ILLEGALLY USED DRUGS

Substances with abuse potential range from simple kitchen spices through common flowers and weeds to highly sophisticated drugs. All these substances may be divided into four categories: (1) depressants (downers), (2) stimulants (uppers), (3) halluc- inogens (psychodelics), and (4) cannabis.

Whatever their classification, most of these drugs have important legitimate applications. Narcotic, sedative, tran- quilizing, and stimulant drugs are essential to the practice of modern medicine. Hallucinogens are used in medical research. To the abuser, though, these medically useful drugs have a compelling attribute: they affect the nervous system producing a change in his emotional responses or reactions. The abuser may feel intoxicated, relaxed, happy, or detached from a world that is painful and unacceptable to him.

The "Characteristics and Effects" charts contained in this chapter categorize commonly abused illegal drugs according to their respective chemical composition. They are provided as a quick reference for drug identification.

DEPRESSANTS (Downers)

NARCOTICS

Medically defined, narcotics are drugs which produce
insensibility or stupor due to their depressant effect on the
central nervous system. Included in this definition are opium,
opium derivatives (morphine, codeine, heroin), and synthetic
opiates (meperidine, oxycodone, methadone).

MORPHINE-LIKE NARCOTICS (Opiates)

Medical Use. Natural and synthetic morphine-like drugs are
the most effective pain relievers in existence and are among the
most valuable drugs available to the physician. They are widely
used for short-term, acute pain resulting from surgery, frac-
tures, burns, etc., and in the latter stages of terminal ill-
nesses such as cancer. Morphine is the standard of pain relief
by which other narcotic analgesics are evaluated.

The depressant effect of opiates produces drowsiness, sleep,
and a reduction in physical activity. Side effects can include
nausea and vomiting, constipation, itching, flushing, constric-
tion of pupils and respiratory depression.

Manufacture and distribution of medicinal opiates are
stringently controlled by the Federal Government through laws
designed to keep these products available only for legitimate
medical use. One aspect of the controls is that those who
distribute these products are registered with Federal authorities
and must comply with specific record keeping and drug security
requirements.

Abuse. The appeal of morphine-like drugs lies in their
ability to reduce sensitivity to both psychological and physical
stimuli and to produce a sense of well-being. These drugs dull
fear, tension, or anxiety. Under the influence of morphine-like
narcotics, the addict is usually lethargic and indifferent to his
environment and personal situation. For example, a pregnant
addict will usually continue drug abuse despite the fact that her
baby will likewise be addicted and probably die shortly after
birth unless immediate medical treatment is undertaken.

The price tag on the abuse of these drugs is high. Chronic
use may lead to both physical and psychological dependence.
Psychological dependence is the more serious of the two, since it
still operates after drug use has been discontinued. With
chronic use, tolerance develops and ever-increasing doses are
required in order to achieve a desired effect. As the need for
the drug increases, the addict's activities become increasingly
drug-centered. When drug supplies are cut off, characteristic
withdrawal symptoms may develop.

Symptoms of withdrawal from narcotic analgesics include:

o Nervousness, anxiety, sleeplessness.

o Yawning, running eyes and nose, sweating.

o Enlargement of the pupils, "gooseflesh," muscle twitching.

o Severe aches of back and legs, hot and cold flashes.

o Vomiting and diarrhea.

o Increase in breathing rate, blood pressure, and temperature.

o A feeling of desperation and an obsessional desire to secure a "fix."

EXEMPT NARCOTIC PREPARATIONS

Under Federal law, some preparations containing small amounts of narcotics are exempt from the prescription requirement. The reason for their exemption lies in the fact that very large quantities of such preparations would have to be consumed regularly for a considerable time to produce significant dependence. These products include certain cough medicines and paregoric remedies which may be sold in pharmacies without a doctor's prescription. Pharmacists selling exempt preparations must be registered with the Federal Government.

Paregoric: Medical Use. Paregoric, a liquid preparation containing an extract of opium, is used to counteract diarrhea and to relieve abdominal pain.

Cough Syrup: Medical Use. Exempt cough formulas which contain codeine are used to combat the symptoms of respiratory disorders. Codeine is an effective cough suppressant when taken in small doses.

Abuse. Although these preparations are reasonably safe and free of addiction liability when used as directed, they can be abused. Addicts will sometimes turn to paregoric or cough syrups, as well as other drugs, when heroin is in short supply. In some areas, high school students and others are known to abuse paregoric medicines and codeine cough remedies. Of the formulas which have been abused, a number have a high alcohol content. Very probably, this has much to do with their popularity. The alcohol content in some of these products is as high as forty percent.

SEDATIVES

This group of depressants includes a variety of old and new drugs which have a depressant effect on the nervous system. Within this group, the most commonly abused products are the barbiturates.

Medical Use. The first barbituric acid derivative, barbital, was introduced to medicine shortly after the turn of the century. Since that time, over 2,500 barbiturates have been synthesized. Today, only about thirty are widely used medically. The barbiturates are among the most versatile depressant drugs available. They are used for epilepsy, high blood pressure, insomnia, and in the treatment and diagnosis of mental disorders. Also, they are used before and during surgery. Alone, or in combination with other drugs, they are prescribed for almost every kind of illness or special situation requiring sedation. Used under medical supervision, barbiturates are normally safe and effective.

Abuse. Although barbiturate intoxication closely resembles alcoholic intoxication, barbiturate abuse is far more dangerous than alcohol abuse or even narcotic abuse. Unintentional over-dosage can easily occur. Convulsions, which may follow with-drawal, can be fatal. The combination of alcohol and barbitur-ates may result in fatal depression of respiratory and cardio-vascular systems. The barbiturate abuser exhibits slurred speech and staggering gait. His reactions are sluggish. He is emotion-ally erratic and may be easily moved to tears or laughter. Sometimes, he has feelings of euphoria. Because he is prone to stumble or drop objects, he often is bruised and has cigarette burns.

Convulsions, which can be fatal, are an ever present danger with barbiturate withdrawal and distinguish barbiturate from narcotic withdrawal. Narcotic addiction is not characterized by a failure of muscular coordination or by convulsions upon drug withdrawal. Whether or not convulsions occur, there may be a period of mental confusion. Delirium and hallucinations similar to the delirium tremors (DT's) of alcoholism may develop. Delir-ium may be accompanied by an extreme agitation that contributes to exhaustion. The delirium may persist for several days followed by a long period of sleep.

MISCELLANEOUS DEPRESSANTS

A number of nonbarbiturate depressants used medically to induce sleep and for sedation are also capable of being abused. With chronic use of high doses, tolerance, physical dependence and psychological dependence can develop. Withdrawal phenomena occur following abrupt discontinuation of drug abuse. Clinical symptoms and patterns of abuse resemble those observed for barbiturates. Because of their abuse potential, several of these drugs have become subject to the Controlled Substances Act.

TRANQUILIZERS

The term "tranquilizer" refers to a rather large group of drugs introduced since the early 1950's. Unlike barbiturate-type sedatives, tranquilizers are generally used to counteract tension and anxiety without significantly impairing mental and physical function. Many are useful as muscle relaxants.

Through the years, it has been found that some tranquilizers occasionally have been abused. The two drugs most often reported have been meprobamate and chlordiazepoxide. Chronic abuse of these drugs, involving increasingly larger daily doses, may result in the development of physical and/or psychological dependence. Symptoms during misuse and following abrupt withdrawal closely resemble those seen with barbiturates.

Massively abused drugs in this category are the "minor tranquilizers" which include: Valium, Librium, Equanil and Miltown. These are the most widely prescribed drugs in the United States today. They are highly synergistic especially with alcohol. Many overdose deaths are related to Valium/Librium/ Alcohol combinations taken unknowingly. These drugs are the "older generation's" drug of choice after alcohol. It is estimated five percent of the U. S. population over the age of fourteen illegally use these drugs.

STIMULANTS (Uppers)

This group includes drugs which directly stimulate the central nervous system. The most widely known stimulant in this country is caffeine, an ingredient of coffee, tea, cola, and other beverages. Since the effects of caffeine are relatively mild, its usage is socially acceptable and not an abuse problem. The synthetic stimulants such as amphetamine and other closely related drugs are more potent and can be abused. Another dangerous stimulant is cocaine.

AMPHETAMINES

Medical Use. Amphetamines have been available since the early 1930's. First used medically as a nasal vasoconstrictor in treatment of colds and hay fever, amphetamines were later found to stimulate the nervous system. This stimulating activity is the primary basis for its use in medicine today. In the main, amphetamines are used in obesity, where the drug exerts an anti-appetite effect, and to relieve mild depression such as that accompanying menopause, convalescence, grief, and senility. Paradoxically, these drugs tend to calm hyperactive, noisy, aggressive children, thus producing more normal behavior.

Amphetamines may produce a temporary rise in blood pressure, palpitations, dry mouth, sweating, headache, diarrhea, pallor, and dilation of the pupils. Such effects are generally seen only with high doses or as occasional side effects with therapeutic doses. Amphetamine drugs seldom cause death, even in acute overdosage.

Abuse. Amphetamines are stimulants. They increase alertness, dispel depression and superimpose excitability over feelings of fatigue. They also produce an elevation of mood and a feeling of well-being. All these are factors underlying amphetamine abuse and explain their popular name, "pep pill."

Amphetamines are usually taken orally in the form of tablets or capsules. However, there have been reports of intravenous use in which amphetamines are dissolved in water and then injected. With this method of administration, the effects of the drug are felt almost immediately.

Most medical authorities agree that amphetamine use does not produce physical dependence, and there is no characteristic abstinence syndrome upon abrupt discontinuance of drug use. Mental depression and fatigue, however, are frequently experienced after the drug has been withdrawn. Psychological dependence is common and is an important factor in continuance of and relapse to amphetamine abuse. The development of tolerance permits the use of many times the usual therapeutic dose. The abuser is talkative, excitable, restless, and experiences a "high." He suffers from insomnia, perspires profusely, has urinary frequency, and exhibits a tremor of the hands. The abuse of one type of amphetamine, drug-methamphetamine ("Speed") is a problem in some areas. Abusers produce highly intensified effects by "mainlining" the drug through injection.

"Speeding" is a common practice among illegal users of amphetamines. This practice makes the "speed freak" one of the most dangerous drug users possible - both to himself and others. "Speeding" is a cycle lasting several days, sometimes as long as a week, during which the "speeder" "cranks" up several times a day, increasing his frequency and dosage each time. Throughout this period, he sleeps and eats little, if at all. After a couple of days, he begins to "burn out", becoming irritable, suspicious, afraid, and dangerously paranoid. Often he begins to hallucinate bugs crawling under the skin, etc. At this point, he is extremely dangerous to others. At the end of his run, he will crash and sleep for several days. Frequently the "speed freak" will use massive doses of "barbs", tranquilizers, opiates or alcohol to help himself crash more easily. Regardless, after this prolonged sleep, the "speed freak" is severely emotionally depressed, and suicide is a real consideration in many instances.

Amphetamine abuse can lead to a psychosis syndrome. This is a mental disturbance very similar to paranoid schizophrenia which can last up to four months after withdrawal and virtually always requires medical treatment. During the mid 1970's an estimated 500,000 American adults were regular, non-medical, amphetamine users and ranked the problem as equivalent with heroin use.

COCAINE

Cocaine is obtained from the leaves of the coca bush found in certain South American countries. It is an odorless, white crystalline powder with a bitter taste, producing numbness of the tongue. The word "coca" is often confused with "cacao." The two are not related. Cacao is the name of a tree from which cocoa and chocolate are derived.

Medical Use. Cocaine was once widely used as a local anesthetic. Its place in medicine, however, has been largely taken by newer, less toxic drugs.

The stimulant effect of cocaine results in excitability, talkativeness, and a reduction in the feeling of fatigue. Cocaine may produce a sense of euphoria, increased muscular strength, anxiety, fear, and hallucinations. Cocaine dilates the pupils and increases the heartbeat and blood pressure. Stimulation is followed by a period of depression. In over-dosage, cocaine may so depress respiratory and heart function that death results.

Abuse. Cocaine is either sniffed, smoked or, injected directly into the vein. The abuse of cocaine tends to be more sporadic than the abuse of heroin. The intense stimulatory effects usually result in the abuser voluntarily seeking sedation. This need for sedation has given rise to a practice of "speedballing" combining a depressant drug, such as heroin, with cocaine or alternating a drug such as cocaine with a depressant. While not apparently addicting physically there is severe emotional depression and other withdrawal symptoms when the frequent user quits. There is a definite psychological dependence which develops. In addition, the user can experience a reverse tolerance syndrome, whereby he needs lesser amounts of the drug to achieve the desired high. This can easily lead to "coke" overdose manifested by convulsions and respiratory arrest due to the vasoconstrictive effects of cocaine.

HALLUCINOGENS (psychodelics)

Distortions of perception, dream images, and hallucinations are characteristic effects of this group variously called hallucinogens, psychotomimetrics, dysleptics or psychedelics. These drugs include lysergic acid diethylamide (LSD), phen-cyclidine (PCP), mescaline, peyote, psilocybin, dimethyl-tryptamine (DMT) and 5-dimethoxyamphetamine (STP). At present, these drugs have no general clinical use except for research applications.

Cannabis was originally classified as a hallucinogen due to the psychoactive properties of tetrahydrocannibinol (THC), its principle active ingredient. Its control under the Controlled Substances Act is similar to the control imposed on narcotics. Cannabis is currently classified separately because its effects vary widely with the user and the dosage.

Lysergic Acid Diethylamide (LSD)

LSD was synthesized in 1938 from lysergic acid. LSD is the most potent of the hallucinogens. On the illicit market the drug may be obtained as a small white pill, as a crystalline powder in capsules, or as a tasteless, colorless, odorless liquid in ampules. Frequently, it is offered in the form of impregnated sugar cubes, cookies, or crackers. LSD is usually taken orally, but may be injected.

LSD primarily affects the central nervous system producing changes in mood and behavior. The user may exhibit dilated pupils, tremor, elevated temperature and blood pressure, and hyperactive reflexes. Use often causes mild waves of anxiety or paranoia which make the user feel he is insane and brings on a sense of panic.

Tolerance to the behavioral effects of LSD may develop with several days of continued use, but physical dependence does not occur. Although psychological dependence may develop, it is seldom intense. Accordingly, most LSD users will use the drug when available, but do not seem to experience a serious craving when LSD cannot be obtained.

In general, the LSD experience consists of changes in perception, thought, mood, and activity. Perceptual changes involve the senses of sight, hearing, touch, body image, and time. Colors seem to intensify or change, shape and space relation appear distorted, objects seem to pulsate, two dimensional objects appear to become three dimensional, and inanimate objects seem to assume emotional import. Sensitivity to sound increases, but the source of the sound is elusive. Conversations can be heard but may not be comprehended. There may be auditory hallucinations of music and voices. There may be changes in taste and food may feel gritty. Cloth seems to change texture, becoming coarse and dry or fine and velvety. The subject may feel cold or sweaty. There are sensations of lightheadedness, emptiness, shaking, vibrations, and fogginess. Subjects lose awareness of their bodies with a resultant floating feeling. Arms or legs may be held in one position for extended periods of time. Time seems to race, stop, slow down, or even go backwards. Changes in thought include a free flow of bizarre ideas including notions of persecution. Trivial events assume unusual significance and importance. An inspiration or insight phenomenon is claimed by some LSD adherents.

The mood effects of LSD run the gamut. There may be bursts of tears, of laughter, or the user may feel no emotion at all. A state of complete relaxation and happiness, not apparent to an observer, may be experienced. A feeling of being alone and cut off from the world may lead to anxiety, fear, and panic. Accordingly, the LSD session is frequently monitored by an abstaining LSD-experienced friend to prevent flight, suicidal attempts, dangerous reaction to panic states, and impulsive behavior, such as disrobing. There may be a feeling of enhanced creativity, but this subjective feeling rarely seems to produce objective results. After a number of hours, the effects of LSD begin to wear off. Waves of the LSD experience, diminishing in intensity, alternate with periods of no effects at all, until all symptoms disappear. Some fatigue, tension, and recurrent hallucinations may persist long after ingestion of the drug. Psychological changes induced by the drug can persist for indefinite periods.

There is, at present, no approved general medical use for LSD. Some interesting results have been obtained with the drug in certain medically supervised research programs, particularly in the treatment of chronic alcoholism and terminal illness. However, the Food and Drug Administration now takes the position that LSD has insufficient clinical utility to warrant either prescription or nonprescription use. Consequently, LSD is now subject to controls similar to those for any unproven investigational drug. Although it may be true that some individuals have had LSD experiences without apparent ill effect, growing medical evidence shows the drug can cause very serious, and often damaging reactions in many individuals. Bizarre behavior in public, panic, fear, and homicidal and suicidal urges have been reported. Psychotic states have been induced through use of the drug, both with emotionally unstable individuals and with persons in whom no sign of emotional instability had been evident. Although most LSD induced psychotic episodes have occurred in persons initially experimenting with the drug, untoward results have also occurred with "experienced" abusers. Furthermore, "casualties" have happened even when the drug has been taken under supervision, both medical and nonmedical. LSD also can produce delayed psychotic reactions in some individuals. In some instances, hallucinations have recurred for weeks after the drug was taken. There is substantial evidence that LSD can cause genetic damage.

Phencyclidine (PCP)

According to a consensus of drug treatment professionals, PCP now poses greater risks to the user than any other illicit drug. PCP use is generally a result of poly-drug orientation since almost all PCP users also use some other drug.

14

In 1978, the National Institute for Drug Abuse reported 13.9 percent of American youths eighteen to twenty-five years of age admitted multi-PCP use. This is double the 1976 usage data. Drug Abuse Warning Network's data reported a doubling of PCP related emergency room cases between 1974-1976. PCP related deaths also doubled during that period.

PCP is the cheapest and most readily available drug around. It can be taken orally, smoked, snorted or injected. Its illicit production is profitable. Chemicals costing thirty dollars can produce thirty thousand dollars worth of PCP. The illegal drug user can purchase a PCP "hit" much cheaper than a marijuana "joint." PCP is commonly substituted for LSD, heroin, marijuana and "speed" by street dealers to increase the price and profit margin.

In its pure form, PCP is a white crystalline powder that readily dissolves in water. Most PCP contains contaminants resulting from its makeshift manufacture, causing the color to range from tan to brown and the consistency from a powder to a gummy mass. Although sold in tablets and capsules, as well as in powder and liquid form, it is most commonly applied to a leafy material, such as parsley, mint, oregano or marijuana, and smoked.

PCP produces in the user a sense of detachment, distance, and estrangement from his surroundings. Numbness, slurred or blocked speech, and a loss of coordination may be accompanied by a sense of strength and invulnerability. A blank stare, rapid and involuntary eye movements, and an exaggerated gait are among the more common observable effects. Auditory hallucinations, image distortion, as in a fun house mirror, and severe mood disorders may also occur, producing, in some, acute anxiety and a feeling of impending doom, in others, paranoia and violent hostility.

PCP is unique among illicit drugs in its power to produce psychosis indistinguishable from schizophrenia. Although such extreme psychic reactions are usually associated with repeated use of the drug, they have been known to occur, in some cases, after only one dose and to last, or recur intermittently, long after the drug has left the body.

MESCALINE, PEYOTE, PSILOCYBIN, "DMT", "STP"

For centuries, various Indian tribes have used mescaline (derived from the Mexican cactus, peyote) in religious cere-monies. Mescaline is available on the illicit market as a crystalline powder in capsules or as a liquid in ampules or vials. It may also be obtained as whole cactus "buttons" (peyote), chopped "buttons" in capsules, or as a brownish-gray

15

cloudy liquid. The drug is generally taken orally, but may be injected. Because of its bitter taste, the drug is often ingested with tea, coffee, milk, orange juice, or some other common beverage.

Psilocybin is derived from certain mushrooms found in Mexico. It has been used in Indian religious rites as far back as pre-Columbian times. It is not nearly as potent as LSD, but with adequate doses, similar hallucinogenic effects are produced. Psilocybin is available in crystalline, powdered, or liquid form.

DMT (dimethyltryptamine) is a more recent addition to the list of presently abused hallucinogenic agents. Although prepared synthetically, it is a natural constituent of the seeds of certain plants found in the West Indies and South America. Powder made from these seeds is known to have been used as a snuff as far back as the arrival of Columbus in the New World. It is still used by some Indian tribes of South America. DMT produces effects similar to those of LSD, but much larger doses are required. The effects are similar to LSD and psilocybin but last only thirty to sixty minutes.

Some varieties of morning glory seeds are also abused for their hallucinogenic effects. The bizarre behavioral effects produced upon ingestion are probably attributable to LSD-like components.

"STP" clinically labeled (dimethoxyamphetamine) DOM, is another frequently abused hallucinogen. Reportedly the effects of this drug are similar to those of LSD but are much longer lasting, even up to seventy-two hours. Because of several severe adverse reactions to STP, its abuse has rapidly declined. It is now subject to the same legal controls as LSD.

CANNABIS

The technical name of the plant from which all marijuana preparations are derived is Cannabis Sativa (L.), sometimes called Cannabis indica, Indian hemp, or simply hemp. The cannabis plant is native to large areas of the world and its fibers have been used for the manufacture of twine, rope, bags, clothing and paper. The stronger strains of marijuana are smuggled into the U. S. from India and the Near East.

Under the Federal law, "marijuana" is defined to mean all parts of the cannabis plant except for the stalks and sterilized seeds. All other preparations of the plant, whether leaves, flowers, resins (hashish), or chemical extracts, are forms of marijuana. The best known of these is hashish, a concentrated preparation of marijuana. In this country, the term "marijuana" usually refers to a preparation of pulverized leaves, resins, flowers, or a combination of these, also called "pot" or "grass" for smoking in pipes, or "reefers," "sticks," or "joints" when rolled as a cigarette.

Marijuana is not a single, simple substance of uniform type. It consists of varying mixtures of different parts of the plant Cannabis Sativa. Among a number of potent chemical compounds (cannabinoids) found in marijuana, delta-9-tetrahydrocannibinol (THC) is the most potent and causes major psychoactive reactions. The psychoactive properties of marijuana range from virtually nonexistent to decidedly hallucinogenic in its stronger forms and high dosages. Unfortunately, much of the discussion among layman and sometimes in scientific forums ignores this very basic and important fact.

EFFECTS ON THE MIND AND BODY

Marijuana is nearly always used for the express purpose of attaining a "high", a disorienting intoxication. The use of marijuana or hashish produces a variety of mental and physical effects which become more pronounced with chronic use.

In most individuals, low to moderate doses of cannabis produce a sense of well-being (euphoria), a pleasant state of relaxation, altered perception, particularly of distance and time, impaired memory of recent events, and impaired physical coordination. The state of intoxication is usually mild and short-lived (two to three hours for each joint). It is now well recognized that even low doses of marijuana adversely affect driving performance. A complex interaction of changes in reaction time, judgement, the perception of sensory stimuli, and of time account for this impairment.

In some users, a single dose of cannabis can produce adverse reactions ranging from mild anxiety, through panic and paranoia, to an acute psychosis characterized by detachment from reality, delusions, hallucinations or illusions, and bizarre behavior. These reactions occur most frequently in individuals who are under stress, anxious, depressed, or borderline schizophrenic, but can also occur in normal users who inadvertently take much more than their "usual dose".

Physiological changes accompanying marijuana use at "low dosage" levels are generally relatively few. One of the most consistent is an increase in pulse rate. Another is a reddening of the eyes at the time of use. Dryness of the mouth and throat is uniformly reported. Although enlargement of the pupils was an earlier impression, more careful study has indicated that this does not occur. Death directly attributable to the drug's effects is extremely rare even with very high doses.

The effects of the drug on the nervous system and brain are undoubtedly the most profound and constitute the greatest problem for the user and the persons around him. These problems include the possible precipitation of psychotic episodes during which the user becomes mentally unbalanced for varying periods of time. Apathy, lack of concern for the future, and loss of motivation have been described in some heavy users; psychotic and paranoid symptoms in others. These symptoms usually disappear gradually when regular drug use is discontinued, and recur when use is resumed. These reactions are relatively rare, although case studies suggest certain cannabis users may be particularly susceptible. Many psychiatrists are concerned about such reactions in young drug users, because of the possibility that regular use may produce adverse effects on psychological, as well as physical, maturation. This concern applies to the use of all psychoactive drugs by the young. For reasons still unclear, a few users experience spontaneous recurrences of acute intoxication symptoms ("flashbacks") days or weeks after consuming cannabis.

Some of the most significant research findings of recent studies conclude:

o Tetrahydrocannabinol (THC), the most prominent psychoactive component of marijuana, can be found in the body's fatty tissue up to eight days following intake, therefore, cumulative build-up takes place with regular use. Although a large percentage of THC is metabolized during this period, clinical studies have found traces of the drug in fatty tissues up to thirty days for chronic users.

o The effects of marijuana on the body's cardiovascular and pulmonary functions are far more harmful than tobacco. Marijuana contains seventy percent more carcinogens by weight than tobacco. Since the "joint" is smoked to a small butt with deep and concentrated smoke inhalations, the drug produces fifty percent more tar than tobacco, and leaves five times as many carcinogens in the lungs as cigarettes. Two or three "joints" daily appear to produce the same relative lung damage risk as a pack of cigarettes.

o Marijuana eventually can widen the gaps between the nerve endings in the brain. This can disrupt the brain areas associated with emotions, memory formation, and behavioral functions.

o THC exerts a variety of effects on male reproductive functions including: damage to genetic cells, supression of pituitary - testical function (sex hormone release), decreased sperm count, and dysfunction of sexual drives.

o Marijuana deforms white blood cells in the human body.
Once impaired, white blood cells are unable to protect the
individual from infection.

o Marijuana disrupts the female's menstrual cycle,
decreases prolactin, an essential hormone in milk reproduction,
and significantly lowers rates of sexual activity.

o Using marijuana during pregnancy increases the risk for
fetus abnormalities and stillbirths.

o Marijuana can precipitate chromosome breakage and affect
aging. Generally, moderate use (as little as twice a week) may
lead to mutations, tumors, virus disease, anemia, and early
aging. Moderate use can cause as much chromosome breakage in two
years as would normally occur in fifty years.

o Marijuana's interaction with other drugs will speed up
the passage of common medications through the body and will
modify their effect. It also causes medications to lose their
potency and causes toxic reaction when used with caffeine,
amphetamines, barbiturates and tranquilizers.

Marijuana is the drug most commonly abused by Marines;
stimulants ("uppers") and cocaine rank a distant second and third
in preference. These drugs, especially marijuana, are popular
because of their general availability, relative low cost, and the
fact that they lend themselves to group use "social settings."
Marijuana is also the least understood of all illegal drugs.
Studies on the adverse effects of marijuana use, such as those
cited above, are only now reaching the point where findings can
be accurately correlated and scientifically validated. The
general rationalization that marijuana is a "safe" drug, with
effects similar to those of alcohol and tobacco, is simply a
myth! The severity and intensity of its effects vary drastically
with age, health and the vulnerability of the user.

A few final facts about marijuana -- On the average, the THC
potency of today's marijuana is at least ten times stronger than
that of the plants used in 1975. Further, "hash oil," a distil-
late of marijuana, which can be used to impregnate "joints" and
other substances such as tobacco, is becoming more prevalent, and
can increase the THC factor to alarming levels. Based on recent
case studies, the evidence is clear that the use of marijuana is
most frequently an individual's introduction to the illegal drug
culture and the primary stimulus for obtaining stronger, more
dangerous drugs.

ILLEGAL USE OF SOLVENTS

Among nondrug substances frequently encountered in drug
abuse situations are various solvents. For example, the
inhalation of solvent fumes from glue, gasoline, paint thinner,

19

and lighter fluid will produce a form of intoxication. Inhalation is practiced most frequently by youngsters between ten and fifteen years of age and occasionally up to eighteen years. Glue is usually squeezed into a handkerchief or bag which is placed over the nose and mouth. Gasoline and paint thinner fumes may be inhaled directly from tanks and cans. After a number of "drags," the individual experiences excitation and exhilaration resembling the initial effects of alcoholic intoxication. Blurring of vision, ringing ears, slurred speech, hallucinations, and staggering are common. This phase of intoxication lasts from thirty to forty-five minutes after inhalation, followed by drowsiness, stupor, and even unconsciousness of about an hour's duration. Upon recovery, the individual usually does not recall what happened during the period of intoxication.

Present knowledge concerning solvent inhalation indicates that physical dependence can develop with the chronic abuse of these agents, and a tendency to increase the amount inhaled suggests tolerance. Repeated use and relapse to use indicate the development of psychological dependence.

Serious problems can develop from solvent inhalation. The chief dangers of inhaling these substances are death by suffocation due to the overwhelming presence of fumes in a small room or through the use of a plastic bag, the development of psychotic behavior, and the state of intoxication these substances produce. Additionally, a severe type of anemia has been observed in glue-sniffers who have an inherited defect of the blood cells (sickle-cell disease). It is known that many solvents and the ingredients in some types of glue damage the kidneys, liver, heart, blood, and nervous system. Although such adverse effects resulting from inhalation are rare, they remain a distinct possibility.

DEGREES OF ILLEGAL DRUG USE

In general, drug users fall into three main groups. The first group employs drugs for a specific or "situational" purpose: the student who uses amphetamines to keep awake at exam time; the housewife who uses diet pills for additional energy to get through household chores; the Marine who uses amphetamines to keep awake while driving all night to reach home on a "seventy-two" hour liberty.

The second group consists of "spree" users, usually of college or high school age. Drugs are used for "kicks," or just the experience. There may be some degree of psychological dependence, but little or no physical dependence because of the sporadic and mixed pattern of use. Drug "sprees" constitute a defiance of convention, an adventurous, daring experience, or a means of having fun. Unlike hard-core abusers, who often pursue their habit alone or in pairs, "spree" users usually take drugs only in group or social situations.

The third is the "hard-core" addict. His activities revolve almost entirely around drug experiences and securing supplies. He exhibits strong psychological dependence on the drug, often reinforced by physical dependence when certain drugs are being used. Typically, the hard-core addict began drug abuse on a spree basis. He has been on drugs for some time and presently feels that he cannot function without drug support.

Obviously, there is much overlapping between these groups, and a "spree" user or "situational" user may deteriorate to the "hard-core" group. The transition occurs when the interaction between drug effects and personality causes a loss of control over drug use. The drug then becomes a means of solving or avoiding life's problems.

IDENTIFICATION OF DRUGS

A frequently asked question is: How can I recognize illegal drugs from legitimate prescription medicines?

The answer is that no one can effectively identify a drug by sight, taste, or smell as all the drugs discussed, except for marijuana, can be found as tablets, capsules, powders, and liquids in varying colors and shapes. Even marijuana, which is usually smoked, can be found as hashish in candy and cookies. There is also marijuana tea and hash oil available today. Therefore, the best that can be done is to suspect the possibility of illegal use when drugs are found under peculiar circumstances or in the possession of someone exhibiting unusual behavior.

There are no instant tests for identification of most drugs. The only way many drugs can be identified is through a series of complicated laboratory procedures performed by a trained technician. Simple visual inspection cannot be relied upon for drug identification. Many potent drugs which are misused are identical in appearance to relatively harmless drugs, many of which may be readily obtained without a prescription.

PROBLEMS IN ILLEGAL USE IDENTIFICATION

Although drug use in its various forms can produce identifiable effects, almost all such manifestations are, at their onset, identical to those produced by conditions having nothing whatever to do with drug use. Many people use legitimate drugs in accordance with physicians' instructions, but without the knowledge of their associates. For example, such disorders as epilepsy, diabetes, or asthma may require maintenance drug therapy that will produce low-level side effects. Also, a person might become drowsy from ingesting a nonprescription product, such as an antihistamine.

A clue to the possibility of illegal drug use comes when otherwise routine or normal actions become abnormally or excessively persistent. However, when tablets, capsules, or other forms of drugs are found on a person suspected of being an illegal user, they are not necessarily narcotics or other dangerous drug.

COMMON SYMPTOMS OF ILLEGAL DRUG USE

Not all drug related character changes appear detrimental, at least in the initial stages. For example, a usually bored, sleepy person while using amphetamines, may become more alert and thereby improve performance. A nervous, high-strung individual on barbiturates, may become more cooperative and easier to manage. What must be looked for, consequently, are not simply changes for the worse, but any sudden changes in behavior out of character with a person's previous conduct. When such behavioral expressions become usual for an individual, there is always a causal factor. That factor could be illegal drug use.

Other signs which may suggest drug use include sudden and dramatic changes in individual conduct and job performance. Drug users may also display unusual degrees of activity or inactivity, as well as sudden and irrational flare-ups involving strong emotion or temper. Significant changes in personal appearance may be cause for concern, for very often a drug user becomes indifferent to his appearance and health habits.

There are other, more specific signs which should arouse suspicions, especially if more than one is exhibited by a single person. Among them are furtive behavior regarding actions and possessions (fear of discovery), sunglasses worn at inappropriate times and places (to hide dilated or constricted pupils), and long-sleeve garments worn constantly, even on hot days (to hide needlemarks). Of course, close or frequent association with known drug users is always a sign of potential trouble.

Because of the expense in supporting a drug habit, the illegal user may be observed trying to borrow money from a number of individuals. If this fails, he will not be reluctant to steal items easily converted to cash, such as cameras, radios, jewelry, etc. And, if his habit is severe enough to force him to use drugs while on duty, he may be found at odd times in places such as closets, or storage rooms. The addict with a high priced habit will reluctantly but regularly turn to selling drugs to support his habit. Understand, however that this discussion deals primarily with the heroin addict who may easily have a three hundred dollars a day habit. Other Marines who use illegal drugs, other than heroin, on a daily basis may be able to support their habits on three to ten dollars a day.

In addition to these behavioral clues, which are common to most illegal drug users, each form of abuse generally has specific manifestations that help identify those engaged in it. They are as follows:

The Glue/Solvent Sniffer. The glue or solvent sniffer usually retains the odor of the substance he is inhaling on his breath and clothes. Irritation of the mucous membranes in the mouth and nose may result in excessive nasal secretions. Redness and watering of the eyes are commonly observed. The user may appear intoxicated or lack muscular control, and may complain of double vision, ringing in the ears, vivid dreams, and even hallucinations. Drowsiness, stupor, and unconsciousness may follow excessive use of the substances. Discovery of plastic or paper bags or handkerchiefs containing dried plastic cement is usually a telltale sign that glue-sniffing is being practiced.

The Depressant User. The user of a depressant drug, such as the barbiturates and certain tranquilizers, exhibits most of the symptoms of alcohol intoxication with one important exception: there is no odor of alcohol on his breath. Persons taking depressants may stagger or stumble. The depressant user frequently falls into a deep sleep. In general, the depressant user lacks interest in activity, is drowsy, and may appear to be disoriented.

The Stimulant User. The behavior of the stimulant user is characterized by excessive activity. The stimulant user is irritable, argumentative, appears extremely nervous, and has difficulty sitting. In some cases, the pupils of his eyes will be dilated even in a brightly lit place.

Amphetamines have a drying effect on the mucous membranes of the mouth and nose with resultant bad breath that is unidentifiable as to specific odor such as onion, garlic, alcohol, etc. Because of mouth dryness, the amphetamine user licks his lips to keep them moist. This often results in chapped and reddened lips which, in severe cases, may be cracked and raw. Other observable effects are: dryness of the mucous membrane in the nose, causing the user to rub and scratch his nose vigorously and frequently to relieve the itching sensation; incessant talking about any subject at hand; and, often, chainsmoking. Finally, the person who is using stimulant drugs often goes for long periods of time without sleeping or eating and usually cannot resist letting others know about it.

The Narcotic User. Few narcotic users are seen in the Armed Forces because they usually cannot function within the highly structured military environment. However, some individuals may drink paregoric or cough medicines containing narcotics. The presence of such bottles in wastebaskets or trash containers is a clue to this form of abuse. The medicinal odor of these preparations is often detectable on the breath.

Other "beginner" narcotic users inhale narcotic drugs, such as heroin, in powder form. Sometimes, traces of this white powder can be seen around the nostrils. Constant inhaling of narcotic drugs makes nostrils red and raw.

For maximal effect, narcotics usually are injected directly into a vein. The most common site of the injection is the inner surface of the arm at the elbow. After repeated injections, scar tissue ("tracks") develops along the course of such veins. Because of the easy identification of these marks, such narcotic users usually wear long sleeves at odd times. Females some-times use makeup to cover marks. Some males get tattooed on injection sites. Associated with the injection of any drugs under unsterile conditions is the hazard of transmitting malaria and other tropical diseases, hepatitis, and blood poisoning.

The presence of equipment ("works" or "outfit") used in injecting drugs is another way to spot the narcotic user. Since anyone injecting drugs must keep his equipment handy, it may be found on his person or hidden nearby in a locker, washroom, or some place where temporary privacy may be found. The most commonly used instruments and accessories are a bent spoon or bottle cap, a small ball of cotton, a syringe or eyedropper, and a hypodermic needle. All are used in the injection process. The spoon or cap holds the drug in a little water for heating over a match or lighter and the cotton acts as a filter when the drug is drawn through the needle into the syringe or eyedropper. The small ball of cotton ("satch cotton") is usually kept after use because it retains a small amount of drug that can be extracted if the user is unable to obtain additional drugs. The bent spoon or bottle cap used to heat the drug is easily identifiable because it becomes blackened by the heating process.

A drug user deeply under the influence of narcotics usually appears lethargic, drowsy ("on the nod") or displays symptoms of deep intoxication. Pupils of the eyes are often constricted and fail to respond to light.

The Marijuana User. The user of marijuana ("pot") is unlikely to be recognized unless he is heavily under the influence. In the early stages of the drug's effect, when the drug acts as a stimulant, the user may be very animated and appear almost hysterical. Loud and rapid talking with great bursts of laughter are common at this stage. In the later stages of the drug effect, the user may seem to be in a stupor or sleepy.

A marijuana cigarette is often rolled in a double thickness of brownish or off-white cigarette paper. Smaller than a regular cigarette, with the paper twisted or tucked in on both ends, the marijuana cigarette often contains seeds and stems and is greener in color than regular tobacco. Marijuana smokers may be identified by their possession of such cigarettes, often called "sticks," "reefers," or "joints."

Another clue to the presence of "reefers" is the way in which they are often smoked. Typically, such smoking occurs in a group situation. But because of the rapid burning and harshness of the marijuana cigarette, it is generally passed rapidly, after one or two puffs, to another person. The smoke is deeply inhaled and held in the lungs as long as possible. The cigarette is often cupped in the palms of both hands when inhaling to save all the smoke possible. An additional clue to marijuana use is its odor. Similar to that of burnt rope, the odor is readily noticeable on the breath and clothing.

The Hallucinogen User. It is unlikely that persons who use hallucinogenic drugs will do so while on duty. Such drugs are usually used in a group situation under special conditions designed to enhance their effect. Persons under the influence of hallucinogens usually sit or recline quietly in a dream or trancelike state. However, the effect of these drugs is not always euphoric. On occasion, users become fearful and experience a degree of terror which may cause them to attempt to escape from the group.

Hallucinogenic drugs are usually taken orally, except PCP, which is generally smoked. They are found as tablets, capsules, or liquids. Users put drops of the liquid in beverages, on sugar cubes, crackers, or even on small paper wads or cloth. It is important to remember that the effects of LSD may recur days, or even months, after the drug has been taken.

DRUG DEPENDENCE

With repeated use, many drugs cause physical dependence. This is when the body learns to live with the drug, tolerates ever-increasing doses, and reacts with certain withdrawal symptoms when deprived of it. The chronic user must constantly increase the dose in order to obtain an effect equal to that from the initial dose. This phenomenon, called tolerance, represents the body's ability to adapt to the presence of a foreign substance. Complete tolerance may not develop to a drug's toxic effects; therefore, no matter how high the individual's tolerance, an addict may still suffer a lethal dose.

A more important factor in keeping the illegal user enslaved by his habit is the psychic or psychological dependence present in most cases of drug abuse. Psychological dependence is an emotional or mental reliance on the effects of the drug. The abuser not only likes the feeling from the drug and wants to reexperience it, he feels he cannot function normally without the drug. It enables him to escape from reality, from his problems and frustrations. The drug and its effects seem to provide the answer to everything, including disenchantment and boredom. With the drug, all seems well. It is the psychological factor which causes an addict who has been withdrawn from his physical dependence to return to illegal drug use.

All substances with abuse potential can produce changes in behavior, particularly when large amounts are improperly used. The user may be withdrawn and solitary, or sociable and talk-ative. He may be easily moved to tears or laughter. He may be quick to argue or believe that someone is "out to get him." These changes in behavior may be harmless, or may constitute a danger to both the user and society.

Three frequently confused terms encountered in drug abuse discussions are "addiction," "habituation" and "drug dependence." "Addiction" is a state of periodic or chronic intoxication produced by the repeated consumption of a drug. It involves: tolerance; psychological dependence; usually physical dependence; an over-whelming compulsion to continue using the drug; and, detrimental effects on both the individual and his unit. "Habituation" is a condition, resulting from the repeated consumption of a drug, which involves little or no evidence of tolerance, some psychological dependence, no physical dependence, and a desire (but not a compulsion) to continue taking the drug for the feeling of well-being that it produces. Detrimental effects, if any, are primarily on the individual.

Through the years, the terms addiction and habituation have been erroneously used interchangeably, with the result that discussions of drug abuse have been fraught with semantic dif-ficulties. Accordingly, the World Health Organization recently recommended that these terms be replaced by a single and more general term: "drug dependence." Drug dependence is described as the state arising from repeated administration of a drug on a periodic or continuous basis. Since many different kinds of drugs can be involved in drug dependence, the term is further qualified in accordance with the particular drug being used; for example: drug dependence of the morphine type; or, drug dependence of the barbiturate type.

Although it was hoped that the newer terminology involving drug dependence and its various qualifiers would eventually replace the older terms of addiction and habituation, this has not proven practical because the language of laws (international,

national and local) which governs drugs subject to abuse encompasses the terms addiction and habituation. Since it would be difficult to set these laws aside, it appears that all three terms will remain a part of drug abuse terminology, with drug dependence being favored by medically oriented groups, and addiction and habituation being favored in legislative and law enforcement circles.

TERMS ASSOCIATED WITH DRUG USE

In order to understand illegal drugs, their use and associated ill-effects, a knowledge of common terms is necessary. As leaders, we cannot develop an effective drug prevention and education program without a firm grasp of some basic definitions and "slang" associated with illegal drug use.

Definitions:

Drugs. Any chemical substance that produces physical, mental, emotional, or behavioral change in the user. As used in this NAVMC it refers to any of the marijuana, narcotics, dangerous, or illicit drugs defined herein.

Controlled Substance. Any drug or substance listed in the code of Federal Regulation Title 21 Part 308 Schedule of Controlled Substances, which has a stimulant, depressant, or hallucinogenic effect and potential for abuse, but excluding any non-narcotic substance that may, under the Federal Food Drug and Cosmetic Act, be lawfully sold over the counter without prescription.

Illicit Drugs. Drugs prohibited by law or lawful drugs when obtained or used without proper authority.

Dangerous Drugs. Non-narcotic drugs that are habit forming or have potential for abuse because of their stimulant, depressant, or hallucinogenic effect. For purposes of identification and clarification, inhaled substances such as: aerosols, glues, paint thinners, and nail polishes used for the aforementioned effect, are included under this category.

Narcotics. Any opiates, i.e., morphine and codeine.

Drug Abuse. The illegal, wrongful, or improper use of any narcotic substance, marijuana, or dangerous drug, or the illegal or wrongful possession, transfer or sale of the same. When such drugs have been prescribed by competent medical personnel for medical purposes, their proper use by the patient for whom prescribed is not drug abuse.

Drug Abuser. One who has illegally, wrongfully, or improperly used any narcotic substance, marijuana, or dangerous drug, or who has illegally or wrongfully possessed, transferred, or sold the same. Drug abusers are classified further as one of the following:

Drug Experimenter. One who has illegally, wrongfully, or improperly used any narcotic substance, marijuana, or dangerous drug as defined herein, not more than a few times for reasons of curiosity, peer pressure, or other similar reason. The exact number of usages is not necessarily as important in determining the category of user as is the intent of the user. For administrative purposes, determination of the category should be within the judgement of the commanding officer, aided by medical, legal, and moral advice, with information, as available, from investigative sources.

Casual Drug Abuser. One who has illegally, wrongfully, or improperly used any narcotic substance, marijuana, or dangerous drug as defined herein, generally several times, and for reasons of deeper and more continuing nature than those which motivate the drug experimenter. For administrative purposes, determination of this category should be within the judgement of the commanding officer aided by medical, legal, and moral advice, and information provided from investigative sources.

Trafficker. One who illegally sells, transfers, or possesses for sale or transfer any of the proscribed drugs defined herein to another person for personal gain.

Dependence. The condition of being subordinate to or controlled by the use of drugs. Dependence may be physiological or psychological.

Physiological Dependence. Physiological dependence is indicated when withdrawal symptoms are present after abstinence from the chemical substance. Determination of physiological dependence will be made by a medical officer.

Psychological Dependence. Psychological dependence is manifested by a dependence on the chemical substance that does not have a physiological/biochemical basis. Psychological dependence must be demonstrated by a history of civilian or military involvement and cannot be diagnosed based on the unsubstantiated claim of the individual. Psychological dependence must be demonstrated by a life style that is totally centered around obtaining and using drugs. Determination of psychological dependence will be made by a medical officer.

Drug Addiction. The extreme form of physical dependence upon drugs. Drug addiction is characterized by physiological damage to the individual, onset of withdrawal syndrome if the use of drugs is discontinued, and a tendency toward further deterioration if the use of drugs is continued.

Tolerance. A physiological phenomenon requiring the individual to use increasing amounts of a drug in repeated efforts to achieve the same effect.

Flashback. Usually precipitated by hallucinogenic drugs. It is a reoccurrence of some features associated with a previous hallucinatory experience, some days or months after the last dose.

Paraphernalia. All equipment, products, and materials of any kind that are used, intended for use, or designed for use in injecting, ingesting, inhaling or otherwise introducing into the human body marijuana, narcotic substances, or other controlled substances in violation of law. A separate section in this chapter lists common items falling within the definition of drug abuse paraphernalia.

Slang Terminology:

The following terms are commonly used among illegal drug users. Terms associated with drug paraphernalia and particular drugs are not included in this list. They can be found respectively under "Paraphernalia and Its Uses" and in the drug classification charts provided in this chapter. Since slang terminology changes periodically, only the most common terms are referenced below:

"Bad Trips". Unanticipated, negative reactions to a drug.

"Bale". A pound of marijuana.

"Big Man". Drug wholesaler who supplies the drug pusher.

"Candy Man". Drug pusher. (Also "BAGMAN")

"Buzz". A drug induced euphoria. (Also "High", "Loaded", "Ripped").

"Chill". Refusal to sell drugs to an addict suspected of being an informant.

"Cocktail". Inserting and smoking marijuana in a regular cigarette.

"Cube". A sugar cube injected with LSD for oral consumption.

"Dime". A drug quantity selling for ten dollars.

"Dope". Common term for illicit drugs.

"Duster". Tobacco, mint leaves, marijuana or parsley, sprinkled with phencyclidine (PCP) and rolled into a cigarette.

"Fix". Term commonly given to a drug dosage.

"Flunkie". An inexperienced addict who takes large risks in acquiring money for drugs.

"Freebase". A cocaine mixture converted to a paste for smoking. The most toxic form of this drug.

"Garbage". Weak, or highly diluted heroin.

"Hit". A single drag or inhalation of hashish or marijuana smoke. (Also "TOKE")

"Jammed-Up". One who has taken a drug overdose.

"Joint". A marijuana cigarette. (Also: "Reefer", Stick")

"Mainlining". Intravenous drug injection.

"Marijuana Burnout". Refers to the ill-effects of prolonged marijuana use. (i.e., dullness, slow motion, inattentiveness).

"Nickel". A drug quantity selling for five dollars.

"Nod". Refers to the drug induced alternating cycle of dozing and awakening.

"Ounce". Common unit of measurement for hashish or marijuana. (Monetarily, 1 oz of hashish is equivalent to 1 lb of marijuana.)

"Quarter Bag". A drug quantity selling for twenty-five dollars.

"Rat". An informer (Also "CHOTA", "STOOL").

"Roach". The small end of a marijuana cigarette remaining after most of it is smoked.

"Run". A continuous period of amphetamine useage.

"Rush". Initial state of euphoria after a drug is injected.

"Skin Popping". Drug injection under the skin.

"Sniffing". Inhalation of a drug through the nasal passage (Also "Snorting").

"Space Cadet". An individual whose senses have become dulled due to prolonged marijuana use.

"Spaced Out". A drug induced state of being out of touch with surroundings.

"Steamboating". Smoking marijuana through a cardboard tube.

"Square". Someone who does not use drugs.

"Tracks". Scars on the body caused by repeated drug injections.

"Trap". A hiding place for drugs (Also "Stash").

"Trey". A bag of heroin.

"Trip". The state of experiencing a drug's effects.

"Wings". The first intravenous shot.

DRUG PARAPHERNALIA AND ITS USES

There is a wide variety of drug paraphernalia available today. Some devices are home made by the illegal drug user, while the more sophisticated items are procured from commercial sources.

Possession of drug paraphernalia is generally a manifestation of illegal drug use. Leaders must be able to recognize these items in order to maintain an effective drug prevention program. Consequently, it is important to know various drug paraphernalia and its uses.

Due to the changing nature of paraphernalia, it is not possible to provide an all inclusive list; however the following are the most common devices:

"Bag". A small transparent envelope used to pack a measure of heroin.

"Bong". A cylindrical water pipe used to smoke marijuana.

"Carburation Pipe". A pipe equipped with a carburation mechanism whereby the smoke is forced out in an explosive manner.

"Chillum". A clay pipe with short stem used for marijuana smoking.

"Cooker". A small receptacle such as a bottle cap or spoon used to heat up a drug and obtain an injectable solution.

"Cocaine Kit". Commonly used for snorting cocaine. The kit consists of: vials, (for storing drug), spoons, straws (for snorting), mirrors, and razor blades (for scraping powdered cocaine into a line and placing it in a straw for snorting purposes).

"Dessicators". Glass pipes for smoking a converted cocaine mixture ("Freebase").

"Freebase Conversion Kit". A kit containing chemicals which reduce cocaine to a paste (freebase) suitable for smoking.

"Head Shops". Stores specializing in the sale of drug paraphernalia and drug related items.

"Isomerizers". Devices which increase marijuana potency by activating the THC content.

"Nail". A hypodermic needle affixed to a medicine dropper for injection purposes.

"Nasal Irrigator". A device used to reduce nasal membrane damage from cocaine snorting. It also enhances sensations during drug intake.

Plastic or Paper Bags. Used for the purpose of sniffing concentrated inhalent vapors.

"Poppers". Small vials containing drugs.

"Quill". A folded matchbook cover used to sniff a drug.

"Roach Clip". A clip or tweezer used to hold the tail end of a marijuana cigarette (Also "Scoop" and "smoking stone").

"Rolling Machines". Machines adjustable or matched to paper sizes for rolling cigarettes.

"Scale". A balance used to weigh drug quantities for selling purposes.

"Sifters". Devices used to remove twigs and seeds from marijuana during the cleaning and refining process.

"Skin". Cigarette paper used to make a marijuana cigarette (Also: "Rolling Papers").

"Snorters". Items, such as straws and spoons, used for snorting cocaine.

"Spike". A hypodermic needle.

"Stash". A container or place used to store drugs.

"Water Pipe". Is a pipe used in smoking marijuana or hashish, it filters the smoke through water. (Also: "HOOKAH").

"Work Kit". A kit used to convert a drug into a solution and inject it. The "kit" usually consists of: matches, a teaspoon with bent handle or small metal bottle cap, medicine dropper, hypodermic needle, cotton and a tourniquet.

Since pictures of these items will enhance the identification process, procurement of paraphernalia literature is recommended. The following are particularly recommended:

Drugs of Abuse, Marihuana, and the Narcotic Identification Manual. These publications can be requested from sources listed in Chapter 5 of this NAVMC.

LEADERSHIP RESPONSIBILITIES

It must be clearly understood by leaders that their responsibilities encompass more than self-education. It is an integral part of the leader's responsibility to "educate" his Marines. Marines must know not only the ill-effects of illegal drugs, but also the key indicators and symptoms associated with their use. Only a well-informed, "educated" Marine can successfully contribute to the elimination of illegal drugs in our Corps.

CHARACTERISTICS AND EFFECTS OF STIMULANTS

DRUGS	SLANG TERMINOLOGY	RISK OF PHYSICAL DEPENDENCE	RISK OF PSYCHOLOGICAL DEPENDENCE	TOLERANCE	METHOD OF USE
COCAINE	BERNICE,BERNIES,BIG "C",BLOW "C",COKE, DREAM,FLAKE,GIRL, GOLD DUST,HEAVEN DUST,NOSE CANDY, PARADISE,ROCK SNOW,WHITE,LADY, MUJER,PERICO,POLVO BLANCO,ROCK	POSSIBLE	HIGH	YES	INJECTED SNIFFED
AMPHETAMINES	BEANS,BENNIES,BLACK BEAUTIES,BLACKBIRDS, BLACK MOLLIES, BUMBLEBEES,CARTWHEELS CHALK,CHICKEN POWDER, CO-PILOTS,CRANK, CROSSROADS,DEXIES, DOUBLE CROSS,EYE OPENERS,HEARTS,JELLY BEANS,LIGHTNING,MINI- BENNIES,NUGGETS, ORANGES,PEP PILLS, ROSES,THRUSTERS, TRUCK DRIVERS, UPPERS	POSSIBLE	HIGH	YES	ORAL, INJECTED
METHAMPHETAMINE	METH,SPEED, CRYSTAL,BOMBIDA	POSSIBLE	HIGH	YES	ORAL
OTHER STIMULANTS		POSSIBLE	HIGH	YES	ORAL

COMMON EFFECTS	RESULTS OF OVERDOSE OR ADDICTION	WITHDRAWAL SYNDROME
INCREASED ALERTNESS, EXCITATION, EUPHORIA, DILATED PUPILS, INCREASED PULSE RATE AND BLOOD PRESSURE, INSOMNIA, LOSS OF APPETITE. SPEECH DISTURBANCES, IMPAIRMENT OF MUSCULAR COORDINATION. EXTREMELY SUSPICIOUS, PARANOID STATE, DISPLAYS OF AGRESSION, DELUSIONS AND HALLUCINATIONS, BIZARRE AND VIOLENT BEHAVIOR.	AGITATION, INCREASE IN BODY TEMPERATURE, HALLUCINATIONS, CONVULSIONS, COMA, POSSIBLE DEATH.	APATHY, LONG PERIODS OF SLEEP. IRRITABILITY, DEPRESSION, DISORIENTATION.

34

CHARACTERISTICS AND EFFECTS OF NARCOTICS

DRUGS	SLANG TERMINOLOGY	RISK OF PHYSICAL DEPENDENCE	RISK PSYCHOLOGICAL DEPENDENCE	TOLERANCE	METHOD OF USE
OPIUM	OP,PEN,YAN,HOP, TAR,BLACK STUFF	HIGH	HIGH	YES	ORAL, SMOKED
MORPHINE	CUBE,FIRST LINE, GOMA,MORF,MORFINA, MORPHO,MORPHY,MUD HOCUS,MISS EMMA, UNKIE,HARD STUFF, "F",WHITE STUFF	HIGH	HIGH	YES	INJECTED SMOKED
CODEINE	SCHOOL BOY	MODERATE	MODERATE	YES	ORAL, INJECTED
HEROIN	BIG "H",BOY,BROWN, BROWN SUGAR,CABALLO, CHIVA,CRAP,ESTUFFA, H,HEROINA,HOMBRE, HORSE,JUNK,MEXICAN MUD,POLVO,SCAG, SMACK,STUFF,THING, CHINESE RED,DOOJEE, HARRY,POWDER	HIGH	HIGH	YES	INJECTED, ORAL
METHADONE		HIGH	HIGH	YES	ORAL, INJECTED
OTHER NARCOTICS		HIGH	HIGH	YES	ORAL, INJECTED

COMMON EFFECTS	RESULTS OF OVERDOSE OR ADDICTION	WITHDRAWAL SYNDROME
EUPHORIA, DROWSINESS, RESPIRATORY DEPRESSION, CONSTRICTED PUPILS, NAUSEA, SKIN ABSCESSES, LUNG CONGESTION, FALL IN BODY TEMPERATURE, APATHY, REDUCED APPETITE, CONSTIPATION, SHAKING, SWEATING, VOMITING, AND ITCHING IN FACIAL REGION-SCRUM HEPATITIS CAN DEVELOP FROM UNSTERILE INJECTION-AFFECT ON PAIN PERCEPTION AND LESSENING OF INHIBITION	SLOW AND SHALLOW BREATHING, CLAMMY SKIN, CONVULSIONS, NEGATIVE EFFECTS ON THE CENTRAL NERVOUS SYSTEM AND GASTROINTESTINAL TRACT-RESPIRATORY FAILURE, COMA, POSSIBLE DEATH	WATERY EYES, RUNNY NOSE, YAWNING, LOSS OF APPETITE, IRRITABILITY, TREMORS, PANIC, CHILLS AND SWEATING, CRAMPS, NAUSEA. INABILITY TO COPE WITH ENVIRONMENT AND STRESS WITHOUT THE DRUG

CHARACTERISTICS AND EFFECTS OF DEPRESSANTS

DRUGS	SLANG TERMINOLOGY	RISK OF PHYSICAL DEPENDENCE	RISK OF PSYCHOLOGICAL DEPENDENCE	TOLERANCE	METHOD OF USE
BARBITURATES	BARBS, BLOCK BUSTERS, BLUEBIRDS, BLUE DEVILS, BLUES, CHRISTMAS TREES, DOWNERS, GREENDRAGONS, MARSHMALLOW REDS, MEXICAN REDS, NEBBIES, NIMBIES, PEANUTS, PINK LADIES, PINKS, RAINBOWS, RED AND BLUES, RED DEVILS, REDBIRDS, REDS, SLEEPING PILLS, STUMBLERS, YELLOWS, YELLOW JACKETS	HIGH	HIGH	YES	ORAL, INJECTED RECTALLY
GLUTETHIMINDE	C.D., CIBAS	HIGH	HIGH	YES	ORAL
METHAQUALONE	QUAALUDE, QUAS, QUADS, SOAPERS, SOPES, SAPORS, SOPOR	HIGH	HIGH	YES	ORAL
CHLORAL HYDRATE	MICKEY, PETER, KNOCKOUT DROPS	HIGH	HIGH	YES	ORAL RECTALLY
TRANQUILIZERS		HIGH	HIGH	YES	ORAL
OTHER DEPRESSANTS		HIGH	HIGH	YES	ORAL

COMMON EFFECTS	RESULTS OF OVERDOSE OR ADDICTION	WITHDRAWAL SYNDROME
SLURRED SPEECH, VAGUE MEMORY, DISORIENTATION-DRUNKEN BEHAVIOR WITHOUT ODOR OF ALCOHOL. POOR MOTOR COORDINATION. MOOD SWINGS, DELIRIUM. UNINHIBITEDNESS IS A PRIMARY REACTION.	AFFECTS THE CENTRAL NERVOUS SYSTEM. SHALLOW RESPIRATION, COLD AND CLAMY SKIN, DILATED PUPILS, WEAK AND RAPID PULSE, CONVULSIONS, COMA, POSSIBLE DEATH.	SEVERE WITHDRAWAL SYNDROME. ANXIETY, INSOMNIA, TREMORS, CONVULSION. POSSIBLE DEATH.

CHARACTERISTICS AND EFFECTS OF HALLUCINOGENS

DRUGS	SLANG TERMINOLOGY	RISK OF PHYSICAL DEPENDENCE	RISK OF PSYCHOLOGICAL DEPENDENCE	TOLERANCE	METHOD OF USE
LSD	ACID,BEAST,BIG "D", BLUE CHEER,BLUE HEAVEN,BLUE MIST, BROWN DOTS,CALIFORNIA SUNSHINE,CHOCOLATE CHIPS,COFFEE,CONTACT LENS,CUPCAKES,HAZE, MELLOW YELLOWS, MICRODOTS,ORANGE MUSHROOMS,ORANGE WEDGES,OWSLEY,PAPER ACID,ROYAL BLUE, STRAWBERRY FIELDS, SUGAR,SUNSHINE,THE HAWK,WEDGES,WHITE LIGHTNING,WINDOW PANE,YELLOWS,LUCY IN THE SKY WITH DIAMONDS, CUBE	NONE	DEGREE UNKNOWN	YES	ORAL
MESCALINE	BERNS,BUTTONS, CACTUS,MESC,MESCAL, MESCALBUTTONS,MOON, DEVOTE	NONE	DEGREE UNKNOWN	YES	ORAL INJECTED
PSILOCYBIN	MAGIC MUSHROOM, MUSHROOM	NONE	DEGREE UNKNOWN	YES	ORAL
MORNING GLORY SEEDS	PEARLY GATES,GLORY SEEDS,SEEDS	NONE	DEGREE UNKNOWN	YES	ORAL, CHEWED
MDA, STP, DMT, DET	LOVE DRUG,STP, (SERENITY, TRANQUILITY,AND PEACE)	NONE	DEGREE UNKNOWN	YES	ORAL, INJECTED SNIFFED
PCP	ANGEL DUST,DOA (DEATH ON ARRIVAL), HOG,KILLER WEED (WHEN COMBINED WITH MARIJUANA OR OTHER PLANT MATERIAL) PCP, PEACE PILL,CRYSTAL, ROCKET FUEL,ELEPHANT TRANQUILIZER, SUPERGRASS,CRYSTAL CYCLONE,TICTAC	NONE	DEGREE UNKNOWN	YES	ORAL, INJECTED SMOKED
OTHER HALLUCINOGENS		NONE	DEGREE UNKNOWN	YES	ORAL, INJECTED SNIFFED

CHARACTERISTICS AND EFFECTS OF HALLUCINOGENS

COMMON EFFECTS	RESULTS OF OVERDOSE OR ADDICTION	WITHDRAWAL SYNDROME
ILLUSIONS AND HALLUCINATIONS (WITH THE EXCEPTION OF MDA DRUG). POOR PERCEPTION OF TIME AND DISTANCE. BLANK STARING EXPRESSION. DIALETED PUPILS, TREMORS, INCREASED BLOOD PRESSURE, RISE IN BODY TEMPERATURE, ACUTE ANXIETY AND DEPRESSION. USE CAN PRECIPITATE "FLASHBACKS" MOOD SHIFTS. DESCRIPTIONS OF RAPTURE, ECSTASY AND BEAUTY CAN BE ACCOMPANIED BY GLOOM, TERROR, AND FEELING OF ISOLATION. VISUAL EXPERIENCES. USERS ARE FLOODED WITH VISUAL EXPERIENCES. LIGHT IS INTENSIFIED, COLORS ARE VIVID, IMAGES ARE NUMEROUS AND PERSISTENT. "BAD TRIPS". NEGATIVE REACTIONS PRECIPITATED BY THE DRUG. PSYCHOTIC BEHAVIOR LASTING SEVERAL MONTHS OR LONGER. VIOLENT BEHAVIOR AND FEAR OF DEATH.	LONGER MORE INTENSE "TRIP" EPISODES, PSYCHOSIS. STUPOR OR COMA LASTING DAYS OR WEEKS. FEELING OF NUMBNESS, CONVULSIONS, MAJOR MENTAL DISORDERS, POSSIBLE DEATH.	WITHDRAWAL NOT REPORTED.

CHARACTERISTICS AND EFFECTS OF CANNABIS

DRUGS	SLANG TERMINOLOGY	RISK OF PHYSICAL DEPENDENCE	RISK OF PSYCHOLOGICAL DEPENDENCE	TOLERANCE	METHOD OF USE
MARIJUANA	ACAPULCO GOLD, BROCCOLI BUSH, DRY HIGH,GAGE, GANGA,GRASS, GRIFFO,HAY,HEMP HERB,JAY,JANE, MARY JANE,MOTA, MUTAH,POD,POT, PANAMA RED, REEFER,SATIVA, SMOKE,STICK,TEA, WEED,SINSEMILLA, THAI STICKS, COLOMBIAN,THC	DEGREE UNKNOWN	MODERATE	YES	SMOKED, ORAL
HASHISH	BLACK RUSSIAN, HASH,KIF,QUARTER MOON,SOLES	DEGREE UNKNOWN	MODERATE	YES	SMOKED
HASHISH OIL	SMASH	DEGREE UNKNOWN	MODERATE	YES	SMOKED

COMMON EFFECTS	RESULTS OF HABITUAL USE	WITHDRAWAL SYNDROME
EUPHORIA, RELAXED INHIBITIONS, INCREASED APPETITE, DISORIENTED BEHAVIOR, REDDENING OF THE EYES, DRYNESS OF MOUTH, IMPAIRED MEMORY, ALTERED SENSE OF TIME, SLOWED REACTION, IMPAIRED COORDINATION, IRRITABILITY, SWEATING, SLEEP DISTURBANCES, INABILITY TO PERFORM TASKS REQUIRING CONCENTRATION, INCREASED HEART RATE, LOUD TALKING AND BURSTS OF LAUGHTER IN EARLY STAGES OF USAGE.	FATIGUE, PARANOIA, POSSIBLE PSYCHOSIS. PERSISTENT CHANGES IN STRUCTURE OF BRAIN CELLS. AFFECTS MENSTRUAL CYCLE (FAILURE TO OVULATE, SHORTENED PERIODS OF FERTILITY). INFLUENCES LEVEL OF ESTROGEN (PRINCIPAL FEMALE SEX HORMONE) AND PROGESTERONE (REPRODUCTIVE HORMONE). EXPERIMENTS INDICATE THE POSSIBILITY FOR MISCAR-RIAGES AND STILLBIRTHS. DUE TO ITS ABILITY TO CROSS THE PLACENTAL BARRIER IT MAY HAVE A TOXIC EFFECT ON EMBRYOS AND FETUSES. LOWER SPERM COUNT IN MALES. REDUCES LEVELS OF TESTOSTERONE (PRINCIPAL MALE SEX HORMONE). PRODUCES DEFECTIVE AND NON-FUNCTIONAL SPERM.	INSOMNIA, HYPERACTIVITY AND DECREASED APPETITE OCCASIONALLY REPORTED.

CHARACTERISTICS AND EFFECTS OF INHALANTS

DRUGS	SLANG TERMINOLOGY	RISK OF PHYSICAL DEPENDENCE	RISK OF PSYCHOLOGICAL DEPENDENCE	TOLERANCE	METHOD OF USE
NITROUS OXIDE	WHIPPETS	POSSIBLE	MODERATE	POSSIBLE	SNIFFING
BUTYL NITRITE	LOCKER ROOM, RUSH	POSSIBLE	MODERATE	POSSIBLE	SNIFFING
AMYL NITRITE	POPPERS, SNAPPERS	POSSIBLE	MODERATE	POSSIBLE	SNIFFING
CHLOROHYDRO-CARBONS	AEROSOL, CLEANING FLUID	POSSIBLE	MODERATE	POSSIBLE	SNIFFING
HYDROCARBONS	AEROSOL, PROPELLANTS, GASOLINE, GLUE, PAINT THINNER	POSSIBLE	MODERATE	POSSIBLE	SNIFFING

COMMON EFFECTS	RESULTS OF OVERDOSE OR ADDICTION	WITHDRAWAL SYNDROME
EXCITEMENT, EUPHORIA, GIDDINESS, LOSS OF INHIBITIONS, AGGRESSIVENESS, DELUSIONS, DEPRESSIONS, DROWSINESS, HEADACHE, NAUSEA, EXCESSIVE NASAL SECRETION AND WATERING OF THE EYES. POOR MUSCULAR CONTROL (STAGGERING) WITHIN FIVE MINUTES OF EXPOSURE. SLURRED SPEECH, BAD BREATH. INCREASED BEHAVIORAL, EMOTIONAL, AND SOCIAL PROBLEMS.	LOSS OF MEMORY, CONFUSION UNSTEADY GAIT, ERRATIC HEART BEAT AND PULSE, LOSS OF CONSCIOUSNESS, HEART FAILURE. SUFFOCATION BY DISPLACEMENT OF OXYGEN FROM THE LUNGS. DEPRESSION OF THE CENTRAL NERVOUS SYSTEM. POSSIBLE DAMAGE TO THE LIVER, KIDNEYS, BLOOD AND BONE MARROW. POSSIBLE DEATH.	INSOMNIA, DECREASED APPETITE, DEPRESSION, IRRITABILITY, HEADACHE

WAR ON DRUGS CHAPTER III

LEADER

LEADERSHIP

EDUCATION

IDENTIFICATION

ENFORCEMENT & STANDARDS

PROGRAMS

"When fire sweeps the field, nothing keeps a man
from running except a sense of honor, of bound
obligation to the people right around him, of
fear of failure in their sight, which might
eternally disgrace him."
                              --- S. L. A. MARSHALL

    The objective of the Marine Corps' illegal drug prevention
program is to eliminate illegal drug use; not slow it down or
control it, but ELIMINATE it!

    Some past drug prevention programs have been ineffective
because they too frequently lacked leader attention. Many
leaders have cited complex legal and administrative red-tape
associated with illegal user identification and prosecution as
justification for not being able to effectively deal with the
problem. Regardless of what stymied our earlier efforts, the
result was a "laissez-faire" attitude in our ranks concerning the
use of illegal drugs. Further, incidents of illegal drug use
have been reported in the officer and staff noncommissioned
officer corps; and, these incidents are not confined to the
younger, "junior" end of these rank structures.

    Only an intensive, dedicated, thoroughly knowledgeable and
total leadership effort can correct the situation and eliminate
illegal drug use from our Corps. A prime forum for leadership
action in combating illegal drug use is the unit/organizational
drug prevention program. This chapter addresses the four major
elements inherent in effectively establishing such programs:
leadership, enforcement of standards, identification, and
education. There is no ideal mix or formula for welding these
elements into "THE ONE BEST WAY". Based on applicable Marine
Corps orders and considerations presented in this chapter, each
unit/organization must tailor a program to its individual
situation, needs, and resources.

MAKE THE ESTIMATE

    Given the mission of establishing an effective illegal drug
use prevention program, with the final objective being the
elimination of illegal drugs, a good way to start is by making an
estimate of the situation: a logical and orderly examination of
all factors affecting the accomplishment of the mission. In
essence, analyze the four key elements - leadership, enforcement

of standards, identification, and education - of an effective illegal drug use prevention program as they currently exist in the unit. Such an examination must include accurate analysis concerning the existence of an illegal drug use problem, the extent of it, the current unit drug prevention program, and its effectiveness. Consider, for example, some of the following questions when estimating the situation relative to the four major key program elements:

o Is there a Unit Drug and Alcohol Abuse Control Officer (DAACO)? Has he received special education or training in his duties? Is his working knowledge adequate? Has he established staff-working liaison with other unit and higher headquarters DAACOs? Does he have access to the commander? Do the unit leaders work with the DAACO when dealing with drug problems?

o How knowledgeable are unit leaders? What do they know about illegal drugs and drug users? Do they understand Marine Corps policy concerning illegal drug use? Do they know the legal and administrative requirements and processes to be applied in combating illegal drugs...do they know when to use them and how to use them? What special training have they had? Are they totally committed to eliminating illegal drugs from our Corps?

o Do the unit's Marines really understand the physiological and psychological hazards of drug use? Do they fully realize how dangerous illegal drug users are in relation to the unit's readiness and the safety and welfare of their fellow Marines? Is their individual pride and their unit esprit strong enough to direct positive peer pressure against those who use drugs?

o How many illegal drug use incidents have occurred in the unit? Who, when, where? Is there a trend or pattern? What quantities and types of drugs have been seized? How many accidents, AWOLs, UAs, AAPDs, and IHCAs are drug related? What follow-up procedures are established in the unit to properly deal with illegal drug users?

o Are urinalysis tests, marijuana dogs, inspections, searches, and investigative agencies used on a regular basis? Are drug incidents, urinalysis results, drug exemption and other pertinent reports reviewed and analyzed by the commander and other unit leaders for trends and problem areas?

o Are there exchanges of statistical data, successful techniques and procedures, detection leads, and other salient information within the unit, between units, and with higher headquarters and investigative agencies?

o What education materials and programs are
available...within the unit...from other units...from higher
headquarters and external agencies? For whom, or what, are they
designed? Are they current? Are they any good? Are the
materials applicable given the unit's mission and situation?

With the above examples as "starters," logical assumptions
can be made about: the unit's strength of commitment to eliminating
the problem (LEADERSHIP); the unit's capability to discern the
extent of its drug problem (IDENTIFICATION); its capacity to
identify and isolate causes of the problem and contributors to
the problem (ENFORCEMENT OF STANDARDS); and, the unit's level of
knowledge concerning the problem and how to deal with it (EDUCATION).
As in combat operations, making the estimate is a continuous
function. It allows for the determination of the most suitable
courses of action, serves as the basis for decisions affecting
procurement and allocation of basic resources (personnel,
material, time, and money), and indicates the need for necessary
refinements, adjustments, or changes during execution of the
plan.

PROGRAM DEVELOPMENT

Once the estimate has been made, and the unit's readiness
and capabilities to combat illegal drugs have been determined,
action must be taken to develop a thoroughly efficient and
effective illegal drug prevention program, or to further refine
and enhance the existing program. As previously stated, there is
no "ONE BEST WAY" in the design of a sound drug prevention
program. There are, however, some sound recommendations and
proven techniques that should be carefully considered, and
official orders, regulations, and requirements that must be
followed in program development and implementation. These will
be presented in relation to the four key elements of a program.
There is, however, one major requirement which does not neatly
fit into any one specific key program element: All commands down
to the battalion/squadron and separate company/activity must have
a Drug and Alcohol Abuse Control Officer. The DAACO is the
commander's principle staff assistant in matters pertaining to
all aspects of preventing illegal drug use. This officer
transforms the commander's guidance and decisions into a viable
illegal drug use prevention program. The DAACO should be one of
the most effective leaders in the unit.

KEY ELEMENTS

Leadership. A total leadership effort and continuous
attention to all aspects of the program are keys to implementing
effective illegal drug use prevention programs. Leadership by
example, such as participating in urinalysis testing and the
local education information/evaluation programs, is the first
step.

We must remember that we are Marines twenty-four hours a day, and that what our Marines do off-duty is our business. Continuous and total commitment to the spirit as well as fair enforcement of the letter of the law and the Corps' policies are required for a successful program.

Probably the most difficult leadership task is the influencing of peer pressure against illegal drugs. We must generate a spirit of motivation and dedication against illegal drugs, but we must not forget the importance and strength of properly channelled peer pressure.

We must:

o Impress upon Marines the fact that anyone involved with illegal drugs is going to create more work for his brother Marines - either because he is high and not performing to standards, on a treatment program, or being separated from the service.

o Make Marines understand that illegal drug use undermines organizational values and unit readiness.

o Emphasize to Marines how special it is to be a Marine.

o Make it known that Marines do not use illegal drugs.

o Insist on pride, professionalism, and military excellence.

o Demonstrate that loyalty to the Marine Corps and a sense of honor demands intolerance of illegal drug use by Marines.

Do these things as part of the unit's welcome aboard orientation the day a new Marine, officer or enlisted, joins.

Commanders and their subordinate leaders - ALL OF THEIR SUBORDINATE LEADERS - are the key to winning the war against illegal drugs. They must be especially well trained in dealing with the problem:

o Leaders must become thoroughly knowledgeable about illegal drugs and be alert for the signs of illegal drug use:

      1. physical symptoms
      2. behavioral changes
      3. deterioration of work performance
      4. attitudinal changes

o   They must be capable of convincing Marines that illegal drug involvement is fundamentally wrong and destructive to organizational effectiveness.

o   NEGATIVE peer pressure may be the most dominant factor in keeping illegal drugs available in the Corps. Leaders must encourage each Marine to exert positive pressure on fellow Marines to give up illegal drugs. Rather than drugs being the popular thing to do, they must become the unpopular thing to do.

o   Know the administrative and punitive consequences of illegal drug use.

o   Leaders need the ability to change attitudes of Marines towards drugs so that the statement, "Marines take care of their own" does not become just lip service. They must teach Marines they are responsible for their fellow Marine's lives.

o   Leaders must develop statistical data to analyze illegal drug use. There must be an exchange of successful techniques and procedures among subordinate organizations.

o   Leaders must be knowledgeable enough to include illegal drug use and the methods to eliminate it as topics in staff and commander's meetings, officer, SNCO, NCO schools and scheduled informational training periods.

o   Vigorous programs specifically designed to involve Marines in off-duty activities must be developed. Commanders are limited only by their imagination, but some ideas to consider are intramural sports programs and other competitive activities, scheduled unit orientation trips, free unit golf/sailing/bowling lessons, and hunting and fishing trips. The Commandant has even mentioned some future expanded recreational facilities such as cable T.V. (HBO) and attractive, new, video game centers.

A word of caution on these programs - it seems almost traditional that Marine organized recreational activities end with a beer bust. Even though there may be nothing wrong with allowing your Marines to blow off steam in this way, a well controlled keg will help avoid alcohol abuse. Don't run out of soft drinks or skimp on food at such events.

o   Leaders must provide individual attention and follow-up action in every instance of illegal drug use. Marines who are involved in illegal drug use but not separated from the Corps must be allowed to prove themselves. Guard against taking any action that will degrade the individual Marine.

o Aggressive, inter-community programs must be created to combat use of illegal drugs off-base. The days of, "What you do off-base is your own business", are gone if they were ever here. We are still Marines twenty-four hours a day and, without community cooperation, we can't meet our responsibility to take care of our Marines off-base.

o Leaders must become knowledgeable of the legal aspects of combating illegal drugs. It is not enough to conduct a search or inspection, collect illegal drugs, and then be unable to prosecute the guilty parties. A knowledge of proper legal procedures will prevent this problem.

o Finally, Marine Corps formal school programs are available to train key personnel such as your DAACO and counselors.

Leaders have a responsibility to counsel and protect their Marines against illegal drug use. One of the most effective preventive measures is a meaningful illegal drug prevention program. This requires initiative, imagination, sincerity and effectively trained counselors.

Marines selected as counselors must be fully educated and trained for the special counseling techniques required to process illegal drug users. Some of these considerations and requirements are:

o Counselors must consider the individual's personal worth, self-respect, and personal needs.

o Counseling should occur primarily within the unit, using trained counselors from major commands.

o Documentation of counseling efforts is required.

o Stress reorientation of attitudes, instilling of human values, and reintegration within the unit.

o Counseling is initiated after medical examination and treatment.

Identification. Commanders must use every available, lawful means at their disposal to identify Marines involved with illegal drugs.

No person will be accessed into the Marine Corps who acknowledges or whose pattern of drug involvement indicates dependency on drugs. Each prospective Marine, officer and enlisted, will be advised that use of an illegal drug by Marines is not tolerated, and, that they will be urinalysis screened for illegal drugs on or immediately after the thirtieth training day. All those showing the presence of an illegal drug in their system will be processed for separation from the Marine Corps.

Some lawful means available to the commander for identification of Marines involved with drugs are:

o Naval Investigative Service (NIS) and other investigative agencies. These agencies can help with, among other things, undercover agents and working agreements with local authorities.

o Urinalysis testing on a regular basis. This testing not only demonstrates the command's ability to detect illegal drugs but also gets the word out to all Marines that illegal drug use will not be tolerated. Portable urinalysis test kits are available for incident related testing: e.g., suspected drug use associated with a crime or behavior suggesting recent use of drugs. Positive results from the portable urinalysis test must be verified by a certified DoD drug testing laboratory if the sample is to be used for administrative discharge characterization or for disciplinary purposes.

o Marijuana dogs should be used as part of the illegal drug prevention program. A commonly heard complaint is that the use of marijuana dogs is demeaning to good Marines who do not use illegal drugs. Rest assured that "the good Marines" welcome any effort to rid the Corps of illegal drugs.

o Health and welfare inspections should be used as necessary to eradicate illegal drugs in the barracks. Inspectors must be schooled about the legal aspects, methods, and the specific purposes of these inspections.

o Random vehicle searches deter the use of motor vehicles as a safe haven for illegal drugs. (For legalities of conducting health and welfare inspections and random vehicle searches, see Chapter IV of this NAVMC and your SJA).

o All illegal drug related reports must go to the commander for determination of required follow-up action.

o A properly run Voluntary Drug Disclosure Program (MCO 5355.3) can be invaluable to the commander for identifying, not only those Marines who are seeking help for their drug problem, but for identifying other illegal drug users named in voluntary disclosures.

o There are certain observable symptoms and characteristics of illegal drug users, as well as terminology and slang which they use. Chapter II of this NAVMC provides information in this area.

Enforcement of Standards. Acceptance of the established standard begins within the officer ranks and is manifested through leadership by example. In this regard, any use of illegal drugs by leaders would be particularly damaging to the overall effort of eliminating drug use in the Marine Corps. Therefore, commissioned officers and warrant officers who use illegal drugs are processed for separation under other than honorable conditions. Trial by courts-martial will be directed when appropriate.

An enlisted Marine who uses or possesses illegal drugs for the first time is subject to appropriate judicial or administrative action. If the Marine's overall conduct/performance record, and the circumstances surrounding the first time drug involvement indicates a potential for continued service, the Marine will be retained in the unit; those first time offenders who are retained undergo a local command course of instruction. Where the review of the Marine's record shows a pattern of misconduct or no potential for continued service, the Marine is processed for separation. Any Marine found using or possessing illegal drugs a second time normally is processed for separation for misconduct, in addition to any nonjudicial or judicial punishment. In special circumstances where the commander determines that the Marine may still have potential for continued service, treatment and further evaluation are provided. No Marine who has been identified using or possessing illegal drugs a third time is retained in the Marine Corps.

The Marine Corps recognizes no responsibility to retain or rehabilitate drug traffickers. The disposition of individuals who traffic in illegal drugs in any amount is accomplished through existing administrative and legal channels.

To determine the acceptance of the established standard, a continuing assessment of the unit's effectiveness in the key areas of leadership and identification is required. Simply stated, it is a continuing estimate of the situation. Assessment allows leaders to recognize the significant aspects of the situation which influence program courses of action, to analyze the impact of all factors upon a particular aspect of the program, and to determine the best employment of available resources to eliminate illegal drug use. Assessment rests on assembling and interpreting information such as:

o Quarterly urinalysis and drug exemption reports.

o Unit illegal drug use incidents.

o Quantities and types of illegal drugs seized from Marines in the unit.

o Results of inspections and searches.

o Reports, formal and informal, from investigative agencies.

In most cases, the assessment will indicate a need for an updating of the command education program.

Education. Marine Corps illegal drug use prevention education takes two forms: Education/Information for all Marines, and Education/Evaluation for identified illegal drug users. Both programs must be continuous, comprehensive, and must actively involve all leaders within the unit. These training programs must be totally accurate and thoroughly credible. Marines already have much misinformation about drugs. Basic to the success of these programs is an honest approach concerning the dangers of illegal drug use. Education should be informative and factual. SERMONIZING MUST BE AVOIDED.

The Education/Information training program for all Marines starts at the Recruit Depots or the Officer Candidates School. Any Marine who attends a formal school at Quantico also receives illegal drug use orientation. Thereafter, in accordance with MCO 5355.1, commanders must provide routine illegal drug use prevention education for all Marines and civilians. Some specific education requirements of the order are as follows:

o Officers and SNCOs must receive illegal drug use education at a new duty station within sixty days of PCS orders and at the discretion of the commander thereafter.

o All Marines and civilian employees not in supervisory positions must receive illegal drug use education within sixty days of reporting to a new duty station and thereafter at the discretion of the commander.

o Civilian employees and DoD dependents at overseas locations must receive illegal drug use education within thirty days of arrival. This education will include all applicable local laws plus an explanation of the program.

o Commanders should make illegal drug use education resources available for dependent school systems.

Although the content and the topic matter in an Education/ Information program are at the commander's discretion, many education and training recommendations are contained in the 1500 and 5728 Marine Corps Bulletin series and Chapters II and V of this NAVMC. This training should help Marines clearly understand values clarification; manifestations of illegal drug use; problem solving; legal aspects of enforcing a drug use prevention program; administrative and punitive consequences of illegal drug use; decision making; and insights into illegal drug use problems.

The purpose of the Education/Evaluation training program for identified illegal drug users with potential for future service to the Corps, is to modify and strengthen individual attitudes against the use of illegal drugs. Additional instructions with which all illegal Drug Education/Evaluation training programs will comply are:

o Marines who use or possess illegal drugs for the first time, who are not drug dependent and who have potential for continued service, will be assigned to a local command course of instruction and evaluation.

o They will remain with their units.

o They will normally perform their regular duties.

o The course will be conducted after normal working hours.

o Unit leaders will participate in all instruction.

o Instructional sessions will be no longer than two hours.

Education/Evaluation programs may consist of subjects and activities the commander feels appropriate, however, course content will emphasize:

o Individual responsibility to unit readiness.

o The importance of individual discipline.

o Development of teamwork, honesty, honor, reliability, and the "Band of Brothers" concept.

o That Marines take care of their own.

o Health hazards to family and personal lives.

o USMC illegal drug policy.

o Legal and administrative consequences of illegal drug use.

This training may involve professional/paraprofessional instructors, such as drug counselors, medical officers, judge advocates, and chaplains, but unit leaders must always be actively involved in the program. The course length is decided by the commander. At the conclusion of the course of instruction, the Marine will be returned to full duty or separated from the service.

If circumstance justify retention of a second time illegal drug user, the Marine must be placed on the major command level treatment program and reevaluated.

SUMMARY

The thrust of the Marine Corps program to eliminate illegal drug involvement rests on leadership, identification, enforcement of standards, and education. Enlightened leadership and acceptance of the established standards are the cornerstones of the Marine Corps program.

Education is provided in two forms: an Education/ Information training program for all Marines; and, an Education/Evaluation training program for identified illegal drug users. Identification is through every legal means available to the commander: urinalysis; investigative agencies; marijuana dogs; inspections; searches; and, the drug disclosure program. The leadership effort has to be total and starts with officers, SNCOs, and NCOs setting the example by active participation in all facets of the war on drugs. There is much guidance, information, and there are many tools for unit commanders to use, but, there remains room for initiative and innovation. Such things as drug hotlines to the commander, local newsletters, drug advisory boards and group assessment of drug statistics and programs can be effective.

Finally, command attention cannot be overstressed. Every individual in the unit must know exactly where the unit leaders stand on illegal drug use and what the consequences are. Officer school, SNCO and NCO schools, and troop information classes are helpful, but nothing works as well as hearing it from the boss. We have our orders -- the final objective is a Marine Corps which is free of illegal drugs.

WAR ON DRUGS CHAPTER IV

LEGAL AND
ADMINISTRATIVE IMPLICATIONS

"A soldier who habitually breaks regulations must be dismissed from the Army. Vagabonds and vicious people must not be accepted for service. The opium habit must be forbidden, and a soldier who cannot break himself of it should be dismissed."

MAO TSE-TUNG
On Guerilla Warfare 1937

Illegal drug use is a violation of the law and illegal drug users are subject to punitive action under the Uniform Code of Military Justice (UCMJ) and/or other appropriate administrative actions. This chapter covers the Marine leader's administrative and legal considerations for effectively combating illegal drug use.

PROCESSING ILLEGAL DRUG USERS

Commanders must give their personal attention to processing every incident of illegal drug use. Commanders should scrutinize all drug related incidents and determine required follow-up action.

DISPOSITION OF ILLEGAL DRUG USERS

Once an illegal drug user is identified, the commander must determine what course of action to follow. Paramount to the success of the program is to hold all Marines accountable for their actions. Each case must be reviewed carefully to include a determination of the individual's potential for continued military service. The following paragraphs are extracted from ALMAR 246-81.

Commissioned Officers and Warrant Officers. It is the policy of the Marine Corps that commissioned officers or warrant officers who use or possess illegal drugs have no potential for further service and will be processed for separation under other than honorable conditions. Trial by court-martial will be directed when appropriate. The position of leadership and responsibility given officers in the Corps demands strict adherence to regulations, and any breach of discipline

54

is considered an extreme violation of special trust and confidence. Paragraph 1100 of the Marine Corps Manual states"...Any offense, however minor, will be dealt with promptly, and with sufficient severity to impress on the officer at fault, and on the officer corps...." All instances of confirmed illegal drug use by an officer will be documented by a special fitness report, regardless of other actions taken.

Staff Noncommissioned Officers and Noncommissioned Officers. Illegal drug use by SNCOs and NCOs is also considered a serious breach of both the law and the special trust and confidence extended to noncommissioned officers. Each instance of illegal drug use involving a noncommissioned officer, especially a staff noncommissioned officer, should be evaluated carefully by commanders to determine the individual's future potential for service. Non-judicial punishment, court-martial, administrative reduction or administrative separation should be administered as appropriate. Special fitness reports will be used to record confirmed instances of drug use for sergeants and above, and special proficiency and conduct marks will be assigned to corporals and below, regardless of other actions taken.

Enlisted Marines. An enlisted Marine found to use or possess illegal drugs the first time is subject to appropriate judicial or administrative action. If the Marine's overall conduct/performance record, and the circumstances surrounding the first time drug involvement indicates a potential for continued service, the Marine will be retained in the unit; those first time offenders who are retained undergo a local command course of instruction. Where the review of the Marine's record shows a pattern of misconduct or no potential for continued service, the Marine is processed for separation. Any Marine found using or possessing illegal drugs a second time normally is processed for separation for misconduct, in addition to any nonjudicial or judicial punishment. In special circumstances where the commander determines that the Marine may still have potential for continued service, treatment and further evaluation will be provided. No Marine who has been identified using or possessing illegal drugs a third time will be retained in the Marine Corps.

Individuals to be Separated. Individuals identified as illegal drug users whose record of service demonstrates consistent poor performance and who are determined to have no potential for future service, will be administratively separated (See MCO P1900.16B (MARCORSEPMAN)). Personnel who have previously been placed in the Voluntary Drug Disclosure Program should be considered as poor risks for retention (See MCO 5355.3).

Drug trafficking is a dishonorable act. The Marine Corps recognizes no responsibility to retain or rehabilitate drug traffickers. The disposition of individuals who traffic in illegal drugs, in any amount, is accomplished through existing administrative and legal channels.

ADMINISTRATIVE ACTIONS

Commanders should exercise their full range of authority and take appropriate administrative action to discourage illegal drug use violations and to ensure Marines are aware of the serious consequences of drug use. Some administrative actions to consider are:

Promotion and Reenlistment. Each Marine must be evaluated on his case alone, and involvement in a drug treatment program does not necessarily deny nor guarantee him promotion or reenlistment. The Marine Corps' policy on promotion and reenlistment will be based upon an individual's demonstrated proficiency and performance, the "whole Marine" concept.

Administrative Reduction. An enlisted Marine may be administratively reduced one pay grade by a commander in accordance with the provisions contained in paragraphs 3000.36 and 4010 of MCO P1400.29B (MARCORPROMAN). This type of reduction is an administrative action designed to increase the efficiency of the Marine Corps, to ensure the integrity of the Marine Corps rank structure, and ultimately to ensure the capability of the Marine Corps to perform its assigned mission. Commanders, as indicated above, may reduce lance corporals and below; however, corporals and above require the convening of a competency board. The Marine would be assigned the date of rank previously held in the grade to which reduced.

Administrative Separation. The use of illegal drugs is specific grounds for administrative separation of enlisted Marines in accordance with MCO P1900.16B (MARCORSEPMAN), as outlined below:

o A discharge for unsuitability may be based on personal use of drugs other than alcoholic beverages.

o A discharge by reason of misconduct may be based on a conviction by civil authorities (foreign or domestic), or action tantamount to a finding of guilty of an offense for which the maximum penalty under the UCMJ is death, or confinement for one year or more; therefore, it is permissible under certain circumstances to award a less than honorable discharge based on a single illegal drug use civil conviction.

o The expeditious discharge is not appropriate in most illegal drug use cases. When illegal drug use is only one element influencing the decision, a commander may direct the discharge, either honorable or general for the convenience of the government.

o Commissioned officers and warrant officers may also be administratively separated in accordance with the provisions of MCO P1900.16B, (MARCORSEPMAN) and SECNAVINST 1920.6. In cases where administrative separation of an officer from the service is being recommended, the commander shall also recommend the type of discharge to be given.

Performance Evaluation System. Any illegal drug involvement by a Marine is a clear violation of the law and the traditional values of the Corps and, therefore, demonstrates a failure of the individual to adhere and live up to the standards required of Marines. All instances of drug use must be recorded by either a special fitness report for sergeants and above or by special proficiency and conduct marks for corporals and below regardless of other action taken.

Officer Qualification Record and Service Record Book Entries. All instances of confirmed illegal drug use must be fully documented in the individual's OQR or SRB.

Duty Status. The commander must review each case carefully and consider all aspects of the individual's duties. It may be necessary to assign an individual duties with increased supervision during the period of treatment to ensure complete evaluation of his potential for further service. If the individual is assigned to duty of a hazardous nature, such as flight, parachute, SCUBA, or EOD, and the commander determines the individual unfit for duty, then his special duty status should be suspended in accordance with MCO P1000.6D (ACTS).

Security Clearance. Identification of a Marine as a illegal drug user creates a question of reliability, but again, it does not require automatic revocation of either his security clearance or access. However, illegal drug use may lead to revocation or suspension of either security clearance or access, and if it does and the Marine is to be retained, his case should be periodically reviewed for possible reinstatement (See OPNAVINST 5510.1F).

Personnel Reliability Program (PRP). Illegal drug use may preclude assignment to or retention in the PRP. If an individual in the PRP is discovered to be an illegal drug user, then a review of his case is required (MCO 5110.7D).

Operation of a Motor Vehicle. The authority to operate government vehicles or the privilege to drive aboard military installations should be revoked or suspended when a commander has reason to believe the individual operator, military or civilian, presents a hazard to himself or others (See MCO 5110.1B).

Transfer. Identification as an illegal drug user does not affect a Marine's eligibility for transfer or reassignment, except individuals pending separation or disciplinary action, and individuals assigned to the Urinary Surveillance Program. Personnel assigned to the Urinary Surveillance Program must remain with their unit until they have completed the full program cycle. If an illegal drug user is transferred and is in a local treatment program, a complete record of his unresolved drug problem will be forwarded to his next commanding officer.

Liberty. The liberty authorization of an illegal drug user may be suspended in support of his off duty attendance in a treatment program.

Other administrative actions for the commander to consider include:

o Seizure of vehicles transporting illegal drugs in accordance with 49 U.S.C. 781-87 Section 782.

o Eviction from family quarters for military families maintaining or using illegal drugs in quarters.

o Use of "off-limits" declarations for civilian areas or businesses where illegal drug use is condoned or encouraged.

o The withdrawal of authorization for unmarried enlisted Marines to live off-base and receive BAQ (own right).

EVALUATION FOR DEPENDENCE

All identified drug users, including personnel requesting conditional immunity, will be evaluated by a medical officer, assisted by a trained counselor when possible, to determine the individual's level of drug dependence. Based on this examination and interview, the medical officer will provide the commander an evaluation of the individual's drug dependence.

PUNITIVE ACTIONS TO CONSIDER

Navy Regulations 1973, Article 1151, specifically prohibits, except for authorized medical purposes, the introduction, possession, use, sale, or other transfer of marijuana, narcotic substance, or other controlled substances by persons in the Naval Service. Commanders must review each case in detail, and then based on the facts, determine the best course of action to pursue: non-judicial punishment (NJP) or trial by court-martial. Generally, Article 92 (Failure to Obey an Order or Regulation) of the UCMJ will cover most illegal drug use violations. Cases involving commissioned officers, warrant officers, staff noncommissioned officers, and noncommissioned officers, must be considered a serious violation of their special trust and confidence and should be referred to trial by court-martial when appropriate.

LEGAL CONSIDERATIONS

The failure to follow the specific legal guidelines and regulations is the most common reason a commander fails to convict a drug user. Often this failure is based on his subordinates' ignorance of the law, and over zealousness when apprehending the illegal drug user. As discussed in the preceding chapters, it is not enough to recognize and understand the effects of illegal drugs. We must know how to enforce the regulations. All Marine leaders must be knowledgeable of the procedures for handling evidence, conducting searches, conducting inspections, and making apprehensions. The following section will cover some of the legal considerations to conduct inspections, searches, seizures, and urinalysis testing properly.

Inspections. The Marine Corps Manual, paragraph 1011, requires commanders to make or cause to be made such inspections as are necessary to evaluate all functional areas of their command, and to keep themselves informed, at all times, of the overall condition of their command. A good inspection plan is a required element in the tactics available to a commander in his war on drugs.

A commander is responsible for the readiness, security, health, welfare, safety, and good order and discipline of the command, its personnel, and equipment. Pursuant to this responsibility, the commander may examine or inspect the whole or part of a unit, installation, vessel, or vehicle, including an examination conducted at exit or entrance points. No probable cause is required as long as the examination or inspection is for the purpose of carrying out the responsibilities stated above. If unlawful weapons, contraband, or evidence of a crime is uncovered in an inspection, it may be seized, and such evidence may be used in disciplinary proceedings. Before an inspection for unlawful weapons or contraband may be conducted, there must be either a reasonable suspicion that such property is present in

the command or the inspection is a previously scheduled
examination of the command.

To be lawful, an inspection for weapons or other
contraband (such as illegal drugs) must be an inspection of the
commander's unit or a part thereof. Additionally, the inspection
should be scheduled far enough in advance to eliminate any
reasonable probability the inspection is being used as a
subterfuge to search a given individual for evidence of a crime
when probable cause is lacking. Although an inspection must be
previously scheduled, the individuals to be inspected do not have
to be notified of the inspection date. All inspections shall be
conducted in a reasonable fashion and may use any material or
technological aid such as, dogs, radar, x-ray, or other agencies.

All contraband and/or evidence of crimes will be
seized, identified, recorded, and safeguarded until it can be
turned over to the proper authorities. A chain of custody record
must be prepared in order to facilitate the introduction of such
evidence at a trial. The Article 31 warning and associated
rights must be given prior to questioning an individual
concerning any discovered evidence. The following are
inspections:

o   Gate inspections.

o   Health and welfare inspections.

o   Unit urinalysis testing.

Searches. Searches for illegal drugs are, under the law,
conceptually no different than other searches and must follow the
same procedures if the evidence obtained is to be introduced in a
trial. Searches may only be authorized by the individual's
commanding officer, or acting commanding officer, except when
they are incident to a lawful apprehension and a search must be
conducted immediately because of exigent circumstances. For
example, in an illegal drug use case where the time lapse in
getting the commander's approval would allow the dissipation of
the evidence in the blood stream. A commander authorizes a
search based on probable cause where there is a reasonable belief
evidence of a crime, unlawful weapons, or contraband will be
found in the place to be searched or on the person to be
searched. It is imperative all searches and seizures be
conducted in strict accordance with the legal guidelines. Any
evidence obtained by an unlawful or unreasonable search and
seizure, and all evidence derived as a result thereof, will be

inadmissable in a trial. Therefore, it is necessary for commanders to ensure their subordinates understand thoroughly the proper procedure for searches to include:

  o Ensuring there is probable cause for the search.

  o Getting the individual's commanding officer's authorization to conduct the search.

  o Conducting the search in a reasonable fashion, not destroying personal property unless absolutely necessary.

  o Maintaining complete records on any seized evidence, indicating ownership, location, quantity, size, description, etc.

  o Maintaining a chain of custody record, and safeguarding the evidence until it is turned over to proper authorities.

  Urinalysis Testing. Properly conducted urinalysis testing can be used by a commander to identify illegal drug users and as evidence in actions under the UCMJ or in administrative procedures. As urinalysis is a form of inspection, commanders must ensure the legal guidelines concerning inspections, searches, and seizures of evidence (bodily fluids in this case) are followed. The results of urinalysis testing may be introduced as evidence to refer an individual for appropriate administrative or disciplinary action when the testing was conducted:

  o As an inspection (Military Rule of Evidence 313)

  o During a proper search (search and seizure of bodily fluids - Military Rules of Evidence 311-317)

  o As part of a valid medical examination as in a flight physical, diving physical, or annual physical (MRE 312(f)). The results of urinalysis testing during a fitness for duty medical examination may not be used against the individual in either administrative or disciplinary actions.

LEADERSHIP RESPONSIBILITIES

  As leaders of Marines we must:

  o Be knowledgeable of the regulations and the legal and administrative procedures.

  o Provide clear guidance to our subordinates through education, counseling, and development of unit orders and SOP's.

o Be firm, fair, and consistent in our decisions concerning illegal drug use violations.

o Instill an aggressive spirit in our subordinates to report all violations.

o Use all appropriate means available, both administrative and punitive, in following-up reports of illegal drug use.

o Never overlook or ignore the problem. ATTACK IT!

WAR ON DRUGS CHAPTER V

EDUCATIONAL/TRAINING MATERIALS

"Untutored courage is useless in the face of
   educated bullets"

                              Major George S. Patton, Jr.
                              Calvary Journal, April 1922

     Current and relevant literature is essential to effective
illegal drug prevention and education programs. It not only
broadens depth of knowledge, but reinforces credibility as well.
This chapter provides the commander with information about
education and training materials and how to obtain them.

     When preparing educational programs of instruction, several
questions should be considered:

        o What is the specific topic to be presented?

                    Illegal drug identification
                    Illegal drug prevention
                    The effects of marijuana

        o Who is the audience?

                    Officers
                    SNCO's
                    Enlisted
                    Civilian employees/dependents

        o What research facilities are available?

                    Libraries
                    Training and Audiovisual Support Center
                    Command Drug & Alcohol Control Office
                    Local civilian or military drug
                    Agencies or facilities

        o What resources are required?

                    Pamphlets
                    Books
                    Films
                    Slides
                    Handouts

o Who is the instructor and what are his qualifications?

> Officer/SNCO/guest lecture
> Level of knowledge
> Experience

o What is the location, method, and time?

> During or after working hours
> Classroom or in the field
> Lecture or guided discussion

Once these questions are answered, it is prudent to coordinate further action with the nearest Drug and Alcohol Control Officer (DAACO).

THE DAACO

MCO 5355.1 requires all commanders of battalions, squadrons, separate companies, or larger organizations to appoint a DAACO in writing. As the commander's representative, the DAACO is responsible for preparing the command's illegal drug prevention and education program. He can provide assistance concerning:

o Materials, both current and consistent with Marine Corps policy.

o Current and available films and video tapes.

o Available research facilities.

The DAACO can also provide addresses of agencies available to assist in researching particular topics. To avoid a duplication of effort, the DAACO should be the point of contact for the collection and procurement of all materials.

INFORMATION RESOURCES

Material concerning illegal drug use and prevention is continually growing. This section lists some of the most practical resources available through Marine Corps and civilian agencies.

MARINE CORPS SOURCES

Publications. Marine Corps publications are procured through the supply system. The Publications Stock List (SL) 1-3, located in the unit/organizational supply office, catalogs current publications including pamphlets relating to illegal drugs. To locate drug related material in the SL 1-3, refer to Section A, 501 Series, for general listings, or Section B, short title, "DRUGS", for an alphabetical listing. Material, once identified by exact title and publication control number (PCN), can be ordered through normal supply channels. Examples of publications available in the supply system are listed in the Publications and Films Index, page 69.

Audiovisual. The Training and Audiovisual Support Training Center (TAVSC) is the activity charged with providing selected films, graphic training aids, and video tapes. Marine Corps Order 3150.3D provides detailed information concerning TAVSC's support responsibilities.

The TAVSC can provide two listings for audiovisual support materials:

    o OPNAVINST 3157.1 (Navy/Marine Corps films).

    o Defense Audiovisual Agency (DAVA) listings
       (DoD films).

From these listings TAVSC can procure training aids locally or via interservice loan. Examples of films available through the TAVSC are listed under "Films" on page 69.

Library. Military and civilian libraries are a primary source for locating books and articles dealing with illegal drugs. Use the card catalog to locate books. Use the periodical indexes to locate articles. Some of the best indexes for finding drug related articles are:

    o Air University Index to Military Periodicals.

    o Education Index.

    o Social Science Index.

    o Reader's Guide to Periodical Literature.

DEFENSE TECHNICAL INFORMATION CENTER (DTIC)

The DTIC, located in Washington, D.C., can provide the unit with research material. This center is a clearinghouse for research and development materials in a variety of areas and is capable of providing technical reports or a bibliographical listing of technical reports on drug abuse.

Many major commands have direct liaison capability with DTIC. If a contact point is not available in the headquarters or local library, commands may obtain a Registration Kit by calling DTIC autovon 284-6871.

Another alternative is to write:

> Breckinridge Library
> (Attn: Librarian)
> Education Center, MCDEC
> Quantico, VA 22134

and request the DTIC Bibliography Request Forms. Research material will be sent to Breckinridge Library and forwarded to the requesting unit.

LOCAL COMMUNITY

The local community is an important resource available in combating illegal drug use. Organizing efforts with local officials is important to ensure a continuous and viable program for the Marine Corps and the local community. Some of the agencies to contact for information on local community programs and resources are:

o   Law Enforcement Departments.

o   Health and Welfare Offices.

o   Local School and Education Agencies.

STATE

Each state has a single agency for the various illegal drug abuse prevention, treatment, and rehabilitation programs. Single State Agencies for Drug Abuse Prevention (SSAs) will provide information on programs and services in your area. See page 72 for SSA addresses.

NATIONAL

o   The U.S. Government Printing Office has material available from all federal agencies. Publication listings can be requested by topic. For information contact:

> Superintendant of Documents
> U.S. Government Printing Office
> Washington, D. C. 20402

Examples of available materials are provided in the Publications and Films Index on page 69.

o   The National Clearinghouse for Drug Abuse
Information, operated by the National Institute on Drug Abuse
(NIDA), provides the latest information on drugs, prevention, and
treatment. Monthly Publications Listings are available on
request. Contact:

    National Clearinghouse for Drug Abuse Information
    Room 10 A-56
    5600 Fishers Lane
    Rockville, Maryland   20857

    Examples of some materials recommended are in the
Publications and Films Index on page 69.

SUMMARY

    Do not limit efforts to only the materials or resources
contained in this NAVMC. Drug education and training materials
are continually being developed. One key to a successful illegal
drug prevention education program is the ability to provide
current materials on a regular basis. Remember to coordinate
with senior and subordinate DAACO's when ordering material to
eliminate costly duplication of effort.

PUBLICATION AND FILMS INDEX

   The following publications and films provide information
relevant to illegal drug education. The materials are basic to
any illegal drug prevention and education program in Marine Corps
organizations.

PUBLICATIONS

   Marine Corps

   o Drug Abuse Prevention For Your Family, PCN 50100210000.
      This pamphlet gives the latest information on the
effects of many commonly used drugs and, most important,
information on how the family can become active and effective
drug abuse preventors.

   o Drug Abuse Prevention For You and Your Friends, PCN
50100211100.
      This booklet is about illegal drugs and preventing drug
problems. It discusses some fairly simple things to do to stop
drugs from becoming a problem.

   o Marijuana Update.
      This pamphlet discusses today's concerns about
marijuana and what marijuana does to the whole person, rather
than just the body organs.

   U. S. Government Printing Office

   o Marihuana, Under the Microscope
      Published by the Drug Enforcement Administration,
Department of Justice, Washington, D.C. This publication
presents the views of ranking officials of the U. S. Government
and private health, research, and treatment organizations on the
health hazards of marijuana.

   o Drugs of Abuse
      Published by the Drug Enforcement Administration,
Department of Justice, Washington, D.C. This publication is
designed to give professionals in the law enforcement, criminal
justice, health, and education fields factual, accurate
information on drug abuse and federal drug laws.

   o Narcotic Identification Manual
      Published by the Bureau of Customs, Department of the
Treasury, Washington, D.C. This manual provides an aid to proper
illegal drug identification. It contains color photographs and
brief narratives relative to each substance shown.

NATIONAL INSTITUTE ON DRUG ABUSE

o Let's Talk About Drug Abuse
        Published by the Special Action Office for Drug Abuse
Prevention in 1975 and revised by the Office of Communications
and Public Affairs, National Institute on Drug Abuse, May 1980.
This pamphlet presents many of the questions about drugs and drug
use that concern adults and young people. The answers to these
questions can be a good beginning for a guided discussion on drug
abuse.

o Parents, Peers, and Pot
        Published by the U.S. Department of Health and Human
Services. This book is about families and drug abuse but is
primarily about the use of marijuana by children. In a day when
self-expression and freedom of choice are common themes, this
book is a reminder to us all about the important role of
providing guidance and exercising discipline for children.

o Marijuana and Health
        The eighth annual report to the U. S. Congress from the
Secretary of Health and Human Services 1980. This report
discusses many recent developments in marijuana research along
with a summary of the scientific research accumulated through the
end of 1979 concerning the drug's possible health implications.

FILMS

Marine Corps Training and Audiovisual Center

o Angel Death (Accession #69249).
        This 1979 film demonstrates physical, emotional,
and psychological effects plus the extreme dangers of the street
drug commonly known as "Angel Dust".

o Drugs and Alcohol: Family and Peer Factors
(Accession #46063).
        This 1979 film discusses attitudes people have
about alcohol and drugs and their influence on family members,
peers, and friends. It examines environmental effects, financial
factors, age groups, prejudices, and constructive/ destructive
behavior experiences by drug and alcohol users.

o Feelin' Good: Alternatives to Drug Abuse (Accession
#46064).
        Narrated by Rev. Jesse L. Jackson, this 1979 film
explores alternatives to drug abuse and presents the human
experience which can be accomplished without drugs and alcohol.
Rev. Jackson relates the mixing of alcohol and drugs to a high
probability of lethal overdose and stresses that "Feelin' Good"
can be achieved by injecting hope in our brains instead of dope
in our veins.

o <u>Alcohol, Pills and Recovery</u> (Accession #52437).
A 1978 film that demonstrates how sedative
hypnotics like alcohol, barbituates, tranquilizers and sleeping
pills affect the body and mind, through an average American
couple raised in the age of anxiety.

o <u>Narcotics File: The Victims</u> (Accession #46666).
A 1974 film that describes various treatment
programs aimed at rehabilitating heroin addicts. It includes
sequences filmed in Hong Kong, Tokyo, Stockholm, London, and New
York dealing with drug free communes, methadone maintenance,
heroin maintenance, harsh jail sentences, one-to-one
psychological treatment and Prison-Cum-Treatment Centers.

ALABAMA
Drug Abuse Program Section
Division of Alcoholism and
Drug Abuse
Department of Mental Health
145 Molton Street
Montgomery, Alabama   36104

ALASKA
Office of Drug Abuse
Dept. of Health & Social
Services
Pouch H-01D
Juneau, Alaska   99801

ARIZONA
Drug Abuse Programs
Division of Behavioral
Health Services
Department of Health Services
2500 East Van Buren
Phoenix, Arixona   85008

ARKANSAS
Office of Drug and Alcohol
Abuse Prevention
Dept. of Social & Rehab.
Services
1515 Building
1515 West 7th
Little Rock, Arkansas   72203

CALIFORNIA
California Department of
Health
Substance Abuse Division
Room 1592, 744 P Street
Sacramento, California   95814

COLORADO
Alcohol & Drug Abuse Division
Department of Health
4210 East 11th Avenue
Denver, Colorado   80220

CONNECTICUT
Connecticut Alcohol and Drug
Council
Department of Mental Health
90 Washington Street
Hartford, Connecticut 06115

DELAWARE
Bureau of Substance Abuse
Governor Bacon Health Center
Cottage #8
Delaware City, Delaware   19706

FLORIDA
Bureau of Drug Abuse Prevention
Division of Mental Health
Dept. of Health & Rehab. Services
1323 Winewood Blvd.
Tallahassee, Florida   32301

GEORGIA
Alcohol and Drug Abuse Section
Div. of Mental Health & Retardation
Department of Human Resources
618 Ponce De Leon Avenue, N.E.
Atlanta, Georgia   30308

HAWAII
Alcohol and Drug Abuse Branch
Department of Health
1270 Queen Emma Street, Room 404
Honolulu, Hawaii   96813

IDAHO
Bureau of Substance Abuse
Division of Community
Rehabilitation
Department of Health & Welfare
LBJ Building, Room 327
Boise, Idaho   83720

ILLINOIS
Dangerous Drugs Commission
300 North State Street, 15th Floor
Chicago, Illinois   60610

INDIANA
Division of Addiction Services
Department of Mental Health
5 Indiana Square
Indianapolis, Indiana   46204

IOWA
Iowa Drug Abuse Authority
615 East 14th Street
Des Moines, Iowa   50319

KANSAS
Drug Abuse Unit
Dept. of Social and Rehab.
Services
Biddle Bldg.
2700 W. 6th Street
Topeka, Kansas 66608

KENTUCKY
Alcohol and Drug Abuse Branch
Division for Prevention
Services
Bureau of Health Services
Department of Human Resources
275 East Main Street
Frankfort, Kentucky 40601

LOUISIANA
Bureau of Substance Abuse
Division of Hospitals
Louisiana Health and Human
Resource Administration
Weber Building, 7th Floor
Baton Rouge, Louisiana 70801

MAINE
Office of Alcoholism and Drug
Abuse Prevention
Bureau of Rehabilitation
32 Winthrop Street
Augusta, Maine 04330

MARYLAND
Drug Abuse Administration
Dept. of Health & Mental
Hygiene
Herbert O'Conor Office Building
201 W. Preston Street
Baltimore, Maryland 21201

MASSACHUSETTS
Division of Drug
Rehabilitation
Department of Mental Health
190 Portland Street
Boston, Massachusetts 02114

MICHIGAN
Office of Substance Abuse
Services
3500 North Logan Street
P.O. Box 30035
Lansing, Michigan 48909

MINNESOTA
Drug and Alcohol Authority
Chemical Dependency Division
Dept. of Public Welfare
402 Metro Square Building
St. Paul, Minnesota 55101

MISSISSIPPI
Division of Drug Misuse
Department of Mental Health
1001 Lee State Office Building
Jackson, Mississippi 39201

MISSOURI
Division of Alcoholism & Drug
Abuse
Department of Mental Health
2002 Missouri Blvd.
Jefferson City, Missouri 65101

MONTANA
Addictive Diseases Division
Department of Institutions
1539 11th Avenue
Helena, Montana 59601

NEBRASKA
Nebraska Commission on Drugs
P.O. BOX 94726
State Captiol Building
Lincoln, Nebraska 68509

NEVADA
Bureau of Alcohol & Drug Abuse
Rehabilitation Division
Department of Human Resources
505 East King Street
Carson City, Nevada 89710

NEW HAMPSHIRE
Office of Drug Abuse Prevention
3 Capital Street, Room 405
Concord, New Hampshire 03301

NEW JERSEY
Division of Narcotic and Drug
Abuse Control
Department of Health
541 East State Street
Trenton, New Jersey 08609

NEW MEXICO
Drug Abuse Agency
Department of Hospitals
& Institutions
113 Washington
Santa Fe, New Mexico   87501

NEW YORK
Office of Drug Abuse Services
Executive Park South
Albany, New York   12203

NORTH CAROLINA
North Carolina Drug Commission
Box 19324
Raleigh, North Carolina 27609

NORTH DAKOTA
Division of Alcoholism
and Drug Abuse
Department of Health
909 Basin Avenue
Bismarck, North Dakota   58505

OHIO
Ohio Bureau of Drug Abuse
Division of Mental Health
Department of Mental Health
and Mental Retardation
2929 Kenny Road, Room B207
Columbus, Ohio   43221

OKLAHOMA
Division of Drug Abuse Services
Department of Mental Health
P.O. Box 53277, Captiol
Station
Oklahoma City, Oklahoma 73105

OREGON
Programs for Alcohol and
Drug Problems
Mental Health Division
Department of Human Resources
2575 Bittern Street, N.E.
Salem, Oregon   97310

PENNSYLVANIA
Governor's Council on Drug
and Alcohol Abuse
Riverside Office Center
Building #1, Suite N
2101 North Front Street
Harrisburg, Pennsylvania 17110

RHODE ISLAND
Rhode Island Drug Abuse Program
Department of Mental Health and
Retardation and Hospitals
303 General Hospital
Rhode Island Medical Center
Cranston, Rhode Island   02920

SOUTH CAROLINA
South Carolina Commission on
Alcohol and Drug Abuse
3700 Forest Drive
P.O. Box 4616
Columbia, South Carolina   29240

SOUTH DAKOTA
Division of Drugs and Substance
Control
Department of Health
Joe Foss Building
Pierre, South Dakota   57501

TENNESSEE
Alcohol and Drug Abuse Section
Department of Mental Health
501 Union Street, 4th Floor
Nashville, Tennessee   37219

TEXAS
Drug Abuse Division
Department of Community Affairs
Box 13166, Capitol Station
Austin, Texas   78711

UTAH
Division of Alcoholism & Drugs
554 South 300 East
Salt Lake City, Utah   84111

VERMONT
Alcohol and Drug Abuse Division
Department of Social & Rehab.
Services
State Office Building
Montpelier, Vermont   05602

VIRGINIA
Department of Mental Health/
Mental Retardation
Division of Substance Abuse
Control
Commonwealth of Virginia
P.O. Box 1797
Richmond, Virginia   23214

WASHINGTON
Office of Drug Abuse Prevention
Community Services Division
DSHS, OB-43E
Olympia, Washington 98504

WEST VIRGINIA
Division of Alcoholism and Drug Abuse
Department of Mental Health
1800 Washington Street, East
Charleston, West Virginia 25305

WISCONSIN
Bureau of Alcohol & Other Drug Abuse
Division of Mental Hygiene
Department of Health and Social Services
One West Wilson Street, Room 523
Madison, Wisconsin 53702

WYOMING
Drug Abuse Programs
State Office Building West
Cheyenne, Wyoming 82001

WAR ON DRUGS - CHAPTER I

PROBLEMS

I.   DRUGS IN SOCIETY

    A.   REASONS MANKIND USES DRUGS

        1.   ALLEVIATE PAIN

        2.   RELIEVE BOREDOM

        3.   ESCAPE STRESS

        4.   CREATE A SENSE OF EUPHORIA

        5.   ENHANCE SOCIAL INTERACTIONS

    B.   OPIUM AND ITS DERIVATIVES

        1.   EARLY USE

        2.   MORPHINE SYNTHESIZED

    C.   ABUSE OF NON-NARCOTIC DRUGS

        1.   IDENTIFICATION

        2.   STATISTICS

II. DRUGS IN THE MARINE CORPS

    A.   DoD SURVEY RESULTS

III. IMPACT OF ILLEGAL DRUG USE

    A.   AFFECTS OF DRUG USE

        1.   INDIVIDUAL

        2.   MARINE CORPS

IV. LEADERSHIP CHALLENGE

    A.   INITIAL TRAINING INDOCTRINATION

    B.   LEADERSHIP REQUIREMENTS

WAR ON DRUGS - CHAPTER II

CLASSIFICATIONS

I.   INTRODUCTION

II.   GENERAL CLASSIFICATIONS OF ILLEGALLY USED DRUGS

    A. DEPRESSANTS

        1. NARCOTICS

        2. SEDATIVES

        3. TRANQUILIZERS

    B. STIMULANTS

        1. AMPHETAMINES

        2. COCAINE

    C. HALLUCINOGENS

        1. LSD

        2. PCP

        3. MESCALINE, PEYOTE, PSILOCYBIN, DMT, STP

    D. CANNABIS

III. ILLEGAL USE OF SOLVENTS

IV.   DEGREES OF ILLEGAL DRUG USE

V.   IDENTIFICATION OF DRUGS

VI.   PROBLEMS IN ILLEGAL USE IDENTIFICATION

VII. COMMON SYMPTOMS OF ILLEGAL DRUG USE

VIII. DRUG DEPENDENCE

IX.   TERMS ASSOCIATED WITH DRUG USE

X.   SLANG TERMINOLOGY OF DRUG PARAPHERNALIA AND ITS USES

XI.   LEADERSHIP RESPONSIBILITIES

WAR ON DRUGS - CHAPTER III

PROGRAMS

I.   INTRODUCTION

II. MAKE THE ESTIMATE

    A. ANALYZE FOUR KEY ELEMENTS

        1. LEADERSHIP

        2. ENFORCEMENT OF STANDARDS

        3. IDENTIFICATION

        4. EDUCATION

    B. MAKING THE ESTIMATE IS CONTINUOUS

III. PROGRAM DEVELOPMENT

    A. NO ONE BEST WAY

    B. DAACO

IV. KEY ELEMENTS

    A. LEADERSHIP

        1. TOTAL AND CONTINUOUS

        2. MARINES 24 HOURS A DAY

        3. INFLUENCING PEER PRESSURE

        4. COMMANDERS AND SUBORDINATES ARE KEY

    B. IDENTIFICATION

        1. ACCESSMENT INTO MARINE CORPS

        2. MEANS AVAILABLE

            a. INVESTIGATIVE AGENCIES

            b. URINALYSIS

            c. MARIJUANA DOGS

            d. INSPECTIONS

C.   ENFORCEMENT OF STANDARDS

    1.   USE OF ILLEGAL DRUGS BY OFFICERS

    2.   USE OF ILLEGAL DRUGS BY ENLISTED

    3.   DRUG TRAFFICKERS

    4.   CONTINUED ASSESSMENT

D.   EDUCATION

    1.   EDUCATION/INFORMATION PROGRAM

    2.   EDUCATION/EVALUATION PROGRAM

V.   SUMMARY

WAR ON DRUGS - CHAPTER IV

LEGAL AND ADMINISTRATIVE IMPLICATIONS

I.   PROCESSING ILLEGAL DRUG USERS

    A.   DISPOSITION OF ILLEGAL DRUG USERS

        1.   COMMISSIONED OFFICERS AND WARRANT OFFICERS

        2.   STAFF NONCOMMISSIONED OFFICERS AND NONCOMMISSIONED OFFICERS

        3.   ENLISTED MARINES

        4.   INDIVIDUALS TO BE SEPARATED

    B.   ADMINISTRATIVE ACTIONS

        1.   PROMOTION AND REENLISTMENT

        2.   ADMINISTRATIVE REDUCTION

        3.   ADMINISTRATIVE SEPARATION

        4.   PERFORMANCE EVALUATION SYSTEM

        5.   OFFICER QUALIFICATION RECORD AND SERVICE RECORD BOOK ENTRIES

        6.   DUTY STATUS

        7.   SECURITY CLEARANCE

        8.   PERSONNEL RELIABILITY PROGRAM

        9.   OPERATION OF A MOTOR VEHICLE

       10.   TRANSFER

       11.   LIBERTY

       12.   OTHER

    C.   EVALUATION FOR DEPENDENCE

    D.   PUNITIVE ACTIONS TO CONSIDER

II. LEGAL CONSIDERATIONS

    A. INSPECTIONS

    B. SEARCHES

    C. URINALYSIS TESTING

III. LEADERSHIP RESPONSIBILITIES